FAMILY MATTERS

A LAYPERSON'S GUIDE TO FAMILY FUNCTIONING

THOMAS A. POWER, ACSW

Hathaway Press
Elan Publishing Company, Inc.
P.O. Box 683
Meredith, New Hampshire 03253

First Printing Fall 1989
Second Printing Spring 1992

Illustrated by Elizabeth Fontaine

Manufactured in the United States of America

CONTENTS

DEDICATION

To My Family

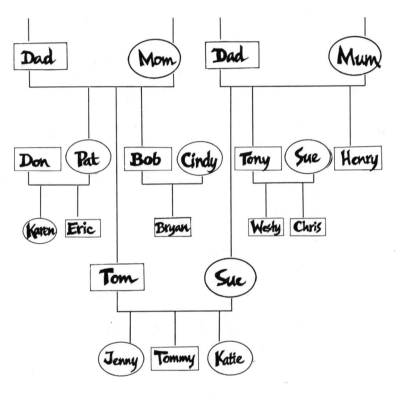

and

To My Wife

Sue

*whose love, support, and partnership create
a presence in my life that provides me with
great joy and abundant strength.*

v

ACKNOWLEDGMENTS

To: *Betty Carter, Director of Family Institute of Westchester, for encouraging and supporting my interest in Community Education and my desire to translate family therapy concepts into the layperson's language.*

To: *All of my colleagues, trainees, and friends at the Family Institute of Westchester for demonstrating commitment and dedication to training the next generation of family therapists and to pursuing new and creative approaches to reduce and prevent family stress.*

To: *The many wonderful teachers and colleagues who have served as catalysts and models for me: Harriet, Eloise, Jerry, Pam, Frank, Monica, Bernard, Kevin, Ken, Burt . . .*

To: *All the families and individuals that I have had the pleasure of working with and learning from.*

To: *Dorothy Daly, aunt extraordinaire, for typing above and beyond the call of duty.*

To: *Ellen Ewens for diligently proofreading the manuscript and for providing creative suggestions that helped to move the book into its final form.*

Thanks!

PREFACE

Family Matters: A Layperson's Guide to Family Functioning is a deliberate attempt to take a look at the family model many of us grew up with and now carry around in our heads. It is written from the vantage point of how our mind thinks about "family," that is, the traditional family of a mother, father, and two children. With both the divorce rate and the re-divorce rate exceeding 50 percent, this imprinted traditional form appears to many as a dream left over from the 40's and 50's. The author has not missed the passage into the night of the traditional family model but rather has chosen to focus neither on this change nor on the social problems that have surrounded it.

The emphasis of *Family Matters* is to make use of this old family model existing in our mind as a way to understand basic family emotional processes. It is extremely useful to understand this blueprint that we have in our heads so that, once understood, we can go forward and apply it to the modern family and its new forms. The purpose of this book is to increase awareness and understanding of the family's emotional processes. This book does not attempt to address the issues surrounding single-parent, remarried, or other family forms. Before that can be done, the building blocks for comprehending the family's emotional processes must first be put in place.

CHAPTER ONE

Understanding Family Therapy Concepts

RECENTLY twenty people defined "family" for me in one word. Admittedly, this was a most unscientific sample because all the participants were either members of my family or friends who happened to be home when I called, but I wanted to get a feel for what various people thought families were all about. Heading the list was "home" with four votes. This was followed closely by "love" with three votes. "Children" and "friends" tied with two votes apiece. "Household," "closeness," "comfort," "Sunday," "group," "nuclear," "vacation," "institution," and "tree" scored one vote each. Some words seemed to have more objectivity than others. "Love" and "comfort" express feelings about families, whereas "group" and "institution" have a sociological flavor. "Sunday" and "vacation" picked up on the time needed to maintain family life. And, although the person who replied "tree" thought he was being funny, he too picked up on another important aspect of "family." Our families were here before us and will continue after us.

To a family therapist, the word that best describes "family," and includes many of the above ideas about the family, is "system." All systems operate in unity for a shared purpose. Family systems originated in biological necessity. Human young are ill-equipped to live in the outside world for many years; they need to be supplied with food, shelter, warmth, protection, love, affection and guidance. While adults can physically care for themselves, they still need a home base, a place where they can feel accepted for who they are, and not what they do and how well they do it. Unlike animals or Mr. Spock, the Vulcan of Starship *Enterprise,* human beings are emotional creatures. They need connections to other human beings, emotional ties, to exist. In fact, few people live totally alone. People without support systems are more vulnerable to every kind of physical and psychological illness, and those people who live alone generally seek some kind of family-like connection with friends, fellow workers, or at church.

Members of healthy families make progress as individuals. These men and women, and their children, are able to function well at work, at school and in their community because they enjoy the confidence and basic security only a happy family can give to the human spirit. People from unhappy families can and do achieve personal success; however, they must overcome the stress of their home environments and endure the loneliness of having no one to share their triumphs.

Thinking about the family as a system developed after World War II, inspired partly by physical and social scientists who were applying systems theory to everything from the economy to the human body. The basic idea of systems theory is that the whole is greater than the sum of its parts. Perhaps the simplest example is the human body. The body is made up of many cells, each with a life force all its own that could conceivably be sustained in another environment besides the body—say a petri dish in a local laboratory—but no one cell in isolation even remotely resembles the miracle of a human life. As individuals, each of us contains our own life force, and as members of a family system each of us has our own specific functions in the family system as well. You act and interact on a daily basis in your job, at school, with friends, as an individual, and experience personal highs and lows, successes and defeats. However, at the same time, you are part of an entire family system of relationships, with each member of that system having the power to affect the others for better or worse.

The word "system" implies interdependence. The individual members of a family system are connected to each other and function together for two common goals: the emotional well-being of the adults and the growth and development of children. This interdependence means that members of a family need each other to get along. Some family members may be more necessary to the unit's physical survival, because they earn the money, or care for children too young to be left alone. But even the most helpless infant is needed emotionally because a child fulfills a parent's dream of having a family. When a child dies, the loss devastates mothers and fathers alike. Even a miscarriage in the first trimester causes a major upset to the prospective parents.

Family members are connected by the things they share and the things they do for one another. The connections between

4

members may be as obvious to the casual observer as their home and numerous possessions, and as invisible as their shared secrets. However, the most important connections are the feelings they have for each other. These feelings are a result of the family ties—or as the saying goes, "Blood is thicker than water." We have feelings about the people at work, or our friends, but family ties make feelings more intense. We react more strongly to what is said or done in the home because we feel that these people are supposed to love us whether we're being lovable or not.

In order for the family system to meet their shared goal—the personal well-being of all its members—they must work together. Of course, there is a paradox inherent in family life. The group is working together to maintain the well-being of each individual member. Each of us has a good idea of what our function is in our family, as well as a good idea of what to expect from other members of the family. These expectations are shared by all members of the system and give us a certain security that leaves us free to carry on our daily lives. Family members do not get up each morning and wonder what they will do that day and how they will do it; they know that someone will help the children get ready for school and someone else will take out the garbage. Nor will they have a family meeting to discuss the merits of eating breakfast together versus eating on the run or not eating at all.

If a change in schedule or duties is required, everyone involved needs to be informed. In this way, a family resembles a corporation that operates to bring about security (in this case, financial) for its employees and stockholders. Corporations require that individuals from different departments maintain constant communication with each other. Various departments report all their equipment and supply needs to the Purchasing Department, and their personnel needs to the Personnel Department. If the Research Department develops a new product, they inform the Marketing Department, which figures out how to sell it. Each bit of communication, every phone call, every memo, spawns another phone call or memo; and when things run well, everyone reacts by doing his or her job.

Most of us encounter "red tape" like this in our work lives or in our dealings with creditors or government agencies. These various systems annoy us with their slowness in getting things done and their seemingly endless capacity for screwing up the details. Yet we all acknowledge that corporations and bureaucracies accomplish things individuals cannot and we put up with the aggravation. Our families too bring "red tape" into our lives. Nobody gets exactly what he or she wants, exactly when he or she wants it. There is a constant "give and take." Of course, it may be less than ideal and, in general, that's what brings people to therapy.

Helping families and individuals achieve better communication—or a better balance in their "give and take"—is the bread and butter of family therapists. However, there really are no trade secrets, and the idea for this book came from my belief that family therapists could make a significant contribution to family well-being by sharing their knowledge with families through an educational vehicle that might help prevent and reduce family stress. Many families are capable of making tremendous gains on their own and families who are already in treatment can make faster progress by having a basic understanding of family systems theory. Essentially, this book is about how families operate and how families might go about achieving a better sense of balance and closeness in their family relationships. It is not meant to be the answer to all family problems. Rather, it is my hope that families, by understanding the principles of family functioning, will be better equipped to cope with the major and minor crises that come with living in an imperfect world. Out of necessity, this book focuses on problems—finding out where problems lie and thinking about alternatives. But, in fact, it might be better to think of problems as tasks or puzzles, or family work. Like other work, family work is challenging, not always pleasant, and rewarding when completed. It is also continuous, which means that it is more important to find a method to solve problems—or do the work—than it is to fix one particular problem.

The family system is in balance when each member acts in a manner agreed upon by all other members of the system. These expectations typically break down into specific roles and responsibilities for the various members. Some of these roles are what sociologists call "instrumental," while others are "expressive." Instrumental roles refer to the concrete tasks necessary for the family system to function—breadwinner, shopper, bill-payer, student, handyman, etc. The expressive roles have to do with either an emotional function in the family—nag, peacemaker, trouble-maker; or a self-image—joker, sexpot. When each family member performs his or her role, or acts the way we expect him or her to act, things chug along smoothly. When one person falls out of line, there is upset.

What a particular family experiences as balance or equilibrium is unique. Balance is not a positive or negative quality and says nothing about how well a family is functioning by anyone else's standards. One family may feel that life is hunky-dory if there is a screaming battle at the dinner table, while another family would not be able to tolerate even the slightest show of hostility without feeling crisis was imminent. In fact, families incorporate many kinds of deviant behaviors—child abuse, spouse abuse, alcoholism, mental illness—into their daily routines or family balance. A professional might assess one family's level of functioning as high and another family's level of functioning as low, but that has little bearing on how the members of a family view their family system. To them, what is best is simply what is familiar.

What brings families in for treatment, in family therapy terms, is a disruption of family balance. One member's behavior typically fails to conform to either the family's or the society's expectations. When the recommendation for treatment comes from an outside agency (e.g., school or court), the behavior has usually been tolerated by the family for a long while. Often a family puts up with an alcoholic member for years and only seeks counseling when the alcoholic is arrested for drunk driving. However, regardless of why a family seeks treatment, the therapist's goal is the same—to help families make positive change.

The first family therapists were practicing psychoanalysts, discouraged about their ability to help patients achieve lasting change. Dr. Murray Bowen and others began to investigate the home environments of patients, and found there was tremendous pressure for them to return to old habits. The patient who may have been able to talk openly with his or her analyst in the hospital or in the analyst's office was unable to bring this new way of thinking back to loved ones who had no similar experience. Seeing families together not only made for faster diagnosis of the patient's problem, it gave other members a chance to air difficulties with each other and with the patient.

7

The general idea was "Where there's smoke, there's fire." The person presented by the family as the troublemaker, or the person who presented himself or herself for treatment, was only the smoke, and meanwhile, back at the ranch, there was a fire. Family therapists came to view the family as the unit of treatment. They agreed that whether or not the person with the complaint—or the person everyone else was complaining about—was a depressed wife or a truant teenager, other family members contributed to creating and maintaining the problem. Family therapy saw problems as existing not in one particular child or in one of the parents, but in the system itself. It also suggested that when there was one problem on the surface there were others which were just as important, if not more so, which were not yet out in the open. To continue the analogy, the goal of therapy was to put out the fire, not just blow away the smoke.

Family therapy emphasizes the family connection rather than the connection of the individual and the therapist. Although a family therapist may work with an individual, the goal is not a long-term attachment, but to zero in on how the family operates as a system. From there the client decides how to go about acting in a way that works better for himself or herself, and prepares to wait for the others to respond in their own way, on their own time schedule. When families come to sessions together—and are all committed to change—the process may be faster, but it's still the same. One change requires other changes—either in behavior or point of view—before everyone again feels they have established a new status quo.

A key to all therapies is the idea of process; or, in plain English, things take time. Process in traditional psychoanalysis involves a person forming an attachment to the analyst and developing a relationship similar to one with parents and gradually breaking away with the blessing of the analyst. In family therapy, the process involves a movement of change throughout the family system. Usually one or more members present a problem, make a change, and gradually other family members absorb the change and react with changes of their own. Technically, the process ends when a new balance has been found. But, in reality, the process is unending because change is a constant factor of family life.

As with many kinds of therapy, the techniques of family therapy were tested and developed with families who had become involved with mental health or law enforcement agencies. However, the ideas are as useful for a family whose chief complaint is a child with study problems as for a family with an alcoholic parent. While those families with more serious problems may need more help in making lasting changes, the principles and methods are the same.

Aside from seeing entire families together, family therapy expanded the definition of "family" to include the nuclear families of both parents. Since our national heritage is one of immigrants and pioneers who often left behind families to establish a new frontier, it may seem unusual to many of us to see our families as playing an active role in our present lives. Many Americans value upward social mobility more than living near family, and people typically pick up stakes several times in a lifetime. It's not unusual to meet a transplanted Ohioan in Texas or to find a couple who have moved three or four times in as many years.

What they leave behind are what family therapists call the "family of origin." These "original families" may be two or two thousand miles away, but they still play a part in our daily lives. Our past experiences with them, and what happens to them in the present, affects us. They taught us how to be a child, a wife or a husband, a mother or a father. Childhood memories become part of our own values and shape beliefs about how things should or should not be done. An argument with a spouse about a savings plan may often be an argument between two different ways of looking at money issues, learned in two different families of origin.

We also have a continuing relationship that ties us to our original families. For example, if an aging parent develops terminal cancer, one must decide how often to visit over the course of the illness, whether you live next door or across the continent. Finite resources like time have to be redirected to face the current problem, which means the spouse and children will be affected. And there is also the worry factor, the emotional strain that comes with impending loss that will affect—at least for a while—the way a person treats the members of his or her nuclear family.

In fact, it is not unusual for a change in the grandparent generation to prompt a change in children or in the marital relationship. Under severe stress in the home, a client may come in complaining about the behavior of a youngster or increased fights with a husband or wife, without mentioning for many weeks some important influence from the original family that started the whole cycle of trouble in the nuclear family.

I'm a firm believer that people don't intentionally go around disappointing those they love, but that all human relationships contain a certain amount of disappointment. Expectations don't fall from the sky; they are learned from our families of origin. We all learn the job of parent and spouse in different training camps, and when we marry and have children we provide a brand new training camp for the next generation. In addition, we carry around inside us a record of how all our past negotiations with our spouses and children have gone. So every current argument or problem is part of a library of how things have gone before. These past expectations play a major role in our current happiness. If others meet our expectations of how we would like them to behave, we feel comfortable. When people disappoint us or don't live up to our expectations, we feel bad. And, just as importantly, if we meet our expectations for ourselves, we feel content and, if we don't, or feel we can't, we feel uncomfortable. One of the goals here is to help you figure out some of the expectations you may have for your spouse and children; how you act when these expectations are not met; and how your original family is influencing your current family. Once you find out how your family system works against your needs—and if it's not good for you it's not good for them either—you can undertake the difficult but rewarding task of trying to change it.

Like most other self-help books, this one is written to what we family therapists would call the "middle generation." This could be taken as a subtle way of pointing the finger at those adults in the prime of their lives, and suggesting that they shoulder responsibility for the problems of their parents and their children as well as themselves. Not only is it written *to* them but also *for* them. Unlike grandparents, adults in the middle generation have direct responsibility for rearing children at the same time that they are going through some of the most stressful growing periods of their own lives. And, unlike children or teenagers, they are more likely to be able to recognize a problem and plan to work on it. A runaway certainly must return home with a mind open to change, but troubled kids need guidance and support from their parents to make changes. Even a young child with a school phobia problem ultimately must realize the need for change but, again, during the hit-and-miss period of acting out the problem, he or she needs parents who firmly insist that there is no choice about going to school. No one can chain a teenager to the house or physically carry a child to school until the age of 16. To get things in the family back on course even the youngest child has to accept the fact that he or she needs a new approach.

At this point I issue a crucial warning. Chances are if you're reading this book you are highly motivated to change—either because you feel your family life could be smoother or you care deeply about maintaining and improving the quality of your family's life. Your challenge will be to read, learn something about where some pitfalls lie, get an idea of how others are playing a part in the difficulties, and then discover that right now you are the only one in the bunch who wants to *do* anything about it. That, too, is part of the process of family life. There will be a lag time before the change is fully taken in and the rest of the family adjusts.

There is also a good chance that anyone reading this book believes that problems need to come out in the open, that families need to talk out difficulties. This value may or may not be true of your spouse and children. You may be contemplating a marvelous image of family togetherness with a spouse who would rather watch TV and teenage children who would prefer to be with their friends. I'm not suggesting that there's no hope, only planting the seed for a lot of patience. When just one family member wants change badly enough, and sticks to a plan for making his or her own change, the others—despite a good deal of kicking and screaming—may follow. The change may not be exactly what you would like or as soon as you would like, but it will happen.

Who Needs Changing: The Problem Bearer?

The key to all change is the ability to recognize the part one plays in the process; this is the most difficult thing to do because it is so much easier to blame others for their part in it instead of looking at one's own role. Often when there is a good deal of stress in a family system, such as when there is sickness, death, parental separation, or loss of job, one family member develops a symptom (like cutting school, abusing alcohol, having an affair, or running away from home). The symptom is a sign that he or she is having a difficult time coping with the emotional upheaval. This individual is considered to be the "problem bearer" (PB).

In any family experiencing the problem, the "PB" is that individual who expresses the problems for the family. We all know the bad guys in the old western movies—they're the ones with the black hats who try to shoot the good guys. In the family system, the bad guys supposedly cause the good guys all the problems. The family presents one member as the problem to be fixed by the therapist. Everyone safely assumes that when this particular person gets it together everyone else can finally relax. Of course, that one person in the family cannot make changes alone. Like it or not, everyone else must change with him or her. Since change is a lot of work and most of us prefer to coast where we can, continually putting the blame on one person saves everyone except the person with the problem a lot of trouble. Like a family mascot, he or she shows the symptom of that stress—for example, a child with school phobia or delinquency, a parent drinking excessively or having an affair. However, blaming one person hinders the development of a family system's way of thinking in that it takes a very narrow and limited view of what is happening in the family. It is vital to look at how the total family is reacting to the stress that exists in their system.

Symptoms tend to surface during periods of high emotional stress and to appear in that family member who is the most vulnerable at that time to the particular stress. Vulnerable does not mean physically weak; rather, it means that person who is most susceptible to the emotional anxiety of the situation. For example, a ten-year-old boy who has been overly close to his mother might develop a symptom (such as vandalism) if his mother were to go back to work. The symptom is a reaction to losing some of the attention he was accustomed to getting from her. Likewise, a man who suddenly lost both of his parents in an auto accident might start drinking excessively as the stress of such a loss overwhelms him. Such symptoms are ways of expressing difficulty in coping with stress. Symptoms do not deal with stress effectively, but are a common emotional sidestepping of real problems. If you were to focus only on the symptoms (vandalism and alcohol abuse) in the above examples, you would only be putting a Band-Aid on a gaping wound because the underlying problems (loss of mother or loss of parents) would not have been dealt with.

It is much more important to try to understand what purpose the symptom serves or what it is trying to cover up. Often, if only the symptom is addressed, it (or one like it) will reappear when the stress again builds to intolerable levels for that particular person. Symptoms often show up in children when parents have marital problems because children are usually quite sensitive to their parents' problems and do not have the skills for coping with them. Thus a symptom can best be defined as an "S.O.S." for the whole family system. It may be that only one family member appears to be having trouble handling the family stress that is either visible or hidden. However, this does not mean that other members of the family are not also feeling the upheaval, but only that the problem bearer is not able to deal with the crisis in a more productive manner and thus develops a symptom.

Symptoms merely mask or distract from the real issues or problems. Ironically, the person identified as the problem bearer—the one we expect to do all the changing—may be the family member least equipped to change at this time. Some family members ignore whatever part they may be playing in the process. If that is what family life is all about, who needs a family! It makes a lot more sense for all family members to stop blaming one person and ask themselves if there is any part they might be playing in maintaining the problem.

What should a family do when a symptom appears in one of its members? The first thing would be to explore and examine all possible options and avenues regarding where the stress might be coming from that is producing the symptom. For example, could the present stress have any connection with the death of a grandmother ten months ago, a sister's recent miscarriage, an impending job re-location, a sibling's acceptance into college, or a brother's marital separation? In looking at the options you need to open your mind to even the most remote possibility. By doing this you are taking a much broader view of what is happening and are moving away from blaming the one with the symptom. After having a better idea of what the stress is and where it is coming from, then try to understand if and how you might be

13

playing some part in contributing to the stress by being over or underinvolved in the situation or by being absent because of numerous work responsibilities.

Let's take the case of a child who appears to be the PB and view her in a broader context. Judy, a thirteen-year-old high school freshman, has just returned from the youth shelter where she had gone after having run away from home. Prior to this, she had recently been cutting school and hanging around with a wild group after school instead of coming home. Judy was labeled "the problem" . . . ungrateful to her parents . . . an irresponsible teenager . . . the PB. After examining the system, I learned that Judy's grandfather committed suicide six months earlier in California and her distraught grandmother wanted to come East to live with Judy's family. Judy's parents have been battling about her grandmother's desire to come East for months. Judy's mother is getting increasingly depressed, sleeping in nearly every morning, and Judy feels that to talk to her parents about her feelings would only make things worse. She fears that her mother might do something "foolish" like her grandfather did. Unable to sort out all of this turmoil, Judy tries to avoid it all by running away.

Obviously, Judy was not the only person in this family experiencing stress and pain; but the symptom (running away from home) surfaced in her at this moment in time because she was the one least able to deal with the anxiety. Running away, however, was not an appropriate solution; it was just Judy's part in the total family problem. Focusing on Judy's behavior alone, without looking at the communications problem between the parents and at the emotional anxiety that was still present in the system as a result of the grandfather's suicide, would not be a good solution either. The best approach is to have everyone take responsibility for his or her part in the family problem. All three people, Judy, her mother, and her father, play a role in the family dilemma and all three must work on their parts if a productive solution is to occur.

Ideally, Judy's parents would be able to see the part that they are playing in this situation; they are not responsible for Judy's running away—only Judy can be responsible for her actions—but if her parents can see the role they play in it, it might spur them to work on their communications problem and thus reduce some of the stress in the system. Judy's running away also serves another purpose in this family. It gets the parents' focus off the grandmother's desire to come East (something that had divided them) and gets their attention onto something that could unite them, namely, their daughter's well-being. This type of behavior should not be viewed as intentional by the PB, but rather as a process that happens in an unknowing way that often works to distract those involved from the more serious issue. The problem with this type of behavior by PB's is that the serious problem between the parents, as in the above case, never gets resolved; it gets put on a back burner only to erupt again at a later date.

The previous example has emphasized how a child can be labeled the PB in a family, but let's not forget that adults can also be narrowly viewed in the same way. For example, the adult with the drinking problem or the spouse who has had an affair usually surfaces as "the problem" when in fact their behavior is symptomatic and an indication that the person is under significant stress and having trouble coping at the present time, and that those who care about him or her must take a broader view of what is happening in the family system and ask what part might he or she be playing in this problem.

Even when an individual volunteers to enter therapy, what is usually asked for is help in coping with the behavior of other family members. Such a person may ask for help, but really sees himself or herself as a victim of the bad guys. The first task in making permanent change is to broaden one's view of the problem. This involves looking within and beyond. By this I mean that each family member must search, or look within, for his or her own role in the problem, and look beyond what appears to be the current surface problem.

Labeling

Being labeled as the source of the family's problem may be the most unfortunate role to have in the family's relationship system, but the "problem bearer" is hardly the only person who wears a label in the family. In fact, all families label all members to some degree, and a member's label is an excellent clue to his or her role within the system.

Labeling becomes an intricate part of the family balance. It

15

often develops as a humorous approach to an issue that has become apparent to everyone, but that no one wants to discuss openly. For example, "Mom's favorite" may be just that, and the other children and Dad may be quite jealous and angry about the whole thing. The name may be bandied about as a joke, while there is a good deal of truth to it. Unfortunately, any one label represents only one truth out of many truths about an individual and binds a person to acting out only one part of his or her personality in all situations.

Labels make us respond to a person in a very narrow and restrictive manner. For example, calling someone a "brain" ignores his or her worries, concerns, and other personality traits. Likewise, the "jock's" feelings and abilities to relate with others might be forgotten with the focus on his athletic prowess. Labeling pigeonholes people; it makes us focus on one aspect of a person to the exclusion of other characteristics.

Figure 1-1
COMMON LABELS

Labels sometimes become self-fulfilling prophecies; that is, label your child "the black sheep," "hellion," or "slob," and your expectations often will be met. The child with the label "hellion" usually gets a lot of attention for disruptive behavior. The "hellion" often has an interesting developmental history; the traits which become a serious problem in adolescence were often present much earlier, but at that time were not considered a problem. The disrespect, the disobedience, and talking back were joked about with phrases such as: "She is just like me, stubborn," "no one is going to tell that child what to do," and "he really gives us a run for our money." Unfortunately, little hellions often grow up to become big problems because the child has had approval for negative behavior.

Everyone plays some part in whatever is happening in a family, and it follows that the person who gets a label contributes in some way to getting and maintaining that label. The person with the label may complain about being labeled, but it is important to look further to see what purpose this label might be serving for him or her. For example, the labeling process might get the child attention and recognition from his or her peers, as well as special attention and pampering at home.

Labels are not always visible or shouted aloud; family members sometimes have a secret sense of what their label is and they act accordingly. These silent labels may be more deadly because they operate beneath the surface. They can be insinuated or implied by the actions of others, as when one child in a family gets the message that "not much is expected of him." Other examples of indirect labels are: "you are not as good as your brother," "I wish you had been a girl," or "you really were a mistake, I didn't want to have any more children." These types of labels are seldom, if ever, said aloud; but they are transmitted into the way people relate with each other.

One woman I know reported that as a youngster she got little response for her straight A's. In early childhood she figured that there was no fuss because good marks were simply expected of her. Both her parents paid more attention to her younger brother's athletic accomplishments. As an adolescent she experimented with shedding her "brain" image with her peers, and when she was a sophomore she brought home her first failing grade, in geometry. She half expected the roof to fall in, or at least to be grounded for a week. What she got was, again, no reaction. The silent message here was that her academic achievement never mattered one way or the other to her parents. They made more of a fuss about what a responsible babysitter she was for her younger brother. This silent message was very powerful, and the woman did not truly enjoy her own academic accomplishments until years later when she returned to graduate school.

Usually labels have negative connotations (brat, dunce); they may also sound positive (genius, sexy), but they are no less restricting. Since all labels limit growth and narrow our perception of someone, it really does not matter whether the label has positive or negative overtones; labeling should be avoided. Most families label to some degree but they often are not aware of the restrictive nature of the process. Labels box people in and limit others from getting a full picture of the total individual.

In the long run, the most positive-sounding label limits individual growth as surely as any negative label. For example, the label "together" means that a person knows how to handle his or her problems. The expectation for the "together" person is that he or she has no problems; therefore, other family members pour out their difficulties to this family sage. However, at a certain point, even the most "together" person experiences a severe disappointment—say, a broken romance or an unexpected death—that puts his or her reserves to the test. When such an incident occurs, the "together" person has had no practice in handling the stress and often has no one with whom to share his or her feelings.

Many of you may have seen *Ordinary People*. This film depicted an entire family which was affluent, successful, and "together" until the accidental drowning of the older son. Like many successful people, we can assume that this fictional family ignored less severe emotional problems by focusing their energies on success and financial security. These things are not bad in themselves, but under a severe stress the family had limited means to cope. The remaining son, being the most vulnerable to the tension and grief because of his age and the fact that he was involved in the accident and lived, attempted suicide.

In other situations, the family "peacemaker"—a cherished role in any family—may become so totally absorbed in the family's problems that he or she neglects to focus on personal development. This self-sacrificing role has its payoffs in the esteem of other family members and the escape it offers from growing into an independent adult with one's own interests. Reading between the lines here you may already be seeing that, contrary to popular opinion, the most "together" person in the family system may be just as troubled as the person who seems to have all the problems.

Chain Reactions

Closely related to the labeling process and balance is the concept of chain reactions. When there is stress or change in the family, each member has a characteristic way of behaving. One person sets the chain reaction in motion and the others follow. What makes us most uncomfortable is our seeming lack of control over our part of the chain. We often feel trapped in a role, forced to play out our part. By identifying our role we can better prepare ourselves for pressure to respond in a certain way and take the initial step toward positive change.

Typically, what is repeated in these situations is the reaction to stress. The cause of the stress may be specific—loss of job, family move, birth—but the individual family member's reaction is generally the same. One family member may handle stress by drinking, another by seeking more time with the spouse, another by being irritable with the ones he or she loves. In other words, in some ways we are all like infants who cry whether they are hungry, wet, dirty, lonely, or just because they need to air their lungs.

What happens in a family system is that our individual responses to stress become part of a chain reaction to stress. So, let's say a particular family system has money problems and both parents are equally concerned about it. The family car breaks down and there is a major, unexpected expense. Both spouses become more tense; they argue; the mother drinks; the father physically abuses the mother; and the adolescent daughter leaves the house. These reactions won't be fixed when the car is fixed. Spending money is a fact of life. This issue—and other stresses—comes up again and again and the cycle of emotional reactions to stress repeats itself over and over.

This example may involve stronger reactions than you have experienced in your own family, but in every family there is a similar process which repeats itself in this way. It may be that

19

when there is a stressful situation one partner withdraws into a good book, leaving the other partner feeling abandoned. This partner may then feel more responsible for the needs of the children and, feeling less support, becomes short-tempered with them. The children, or a particular child, feels the shift and may start acting up to a degree where the parent with the book has simply got to get reinvolved. Once the child ceases acting up again, the bookworm parent withdraws again.

Labels and Identity

Forming an identity occupies a good deal of our time as we are growing up and children respond readily to any sort of label at all. People often carry outgrown labels with them into adulthood and see themselves in the same narrow way their families saw them in childhood. Because labels help us to define ourselves, we hesitate to give them up. This is another reason why change in the family system can be so long in coming. Family members hang onto their labels out of fear of losing part of themselves. Perhaps the closest analogy to the feeling of change would be an emotional amputation.

Let's face it, most people want to be recognized for something, and some will go to great lengths to be noticed for anything. One's label can become a "claim to fame," since every label gives recognition and contributes to one's identity. For example, when the "klutz" arrives on the scene, he doesn't even have to say hello—just stumble into something, knock it down, or fall— and everyone knows that he has arrived and laughs.

Everybody's Problem

Family problems exist in the family system. For example, when a couple is having a marital problem, the problem is not "lodged" or "housed" in either partner, but rather it is between them and gets in the way of their achieving more closeness (*Figure 1-2*). If relationship problems were "in" people, surgery would be the simple solution, but obviously no one goes to a surgeon for a relationship problem.

The trouble with viewing a relationship problem as being "in" somebody else is that it means that one person has total

Figure 1-2

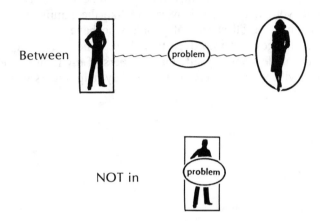

Between

NOT in

responsibility for the problem and the other person has none. That makes one the villain and the other the saint, when it takes *two* to have a problem and keep it going. If one can convince oneself that the problem is "in" the other person, one does not have to change any part of oneself. This is easier, but not an effective way to gain change.

My main goal in writing this book is to help you as a member of a family system to expand your view of who owns the problem and to begin to see what lies between you and those you want to be closer to. Let's begin by building a framework in the next few chapters to help us understand the family as a system. The format of the book is a simple one. In this first chapter, the focus has been on the interconnectedness of family members and the importance, when trying to understand family problems and stress, of changing our camera focus from a zoom (one person) to a wide-angle (family system) lens. In Chapters 2, 3, 4, and 5, we'll look at how problems between people arise and how they are typically handled, for better or worse, and what influences previous generations may have on the nuclear family unit's problems. In later chapters we'll talk about how to make change, and what to expect from those we love when we do.

My training involved learning these same concepts, studying case histories, and working with families. For the most part I have disguised examples from my casework or personal experience to illustrate the concepts of family therapy. Some cases may hit home with you, and others may sound like the family up the street, but they are all stories of people who have faced issues and made changes that improved their lives. They have helped me to better understand myself, the members of my family, and the people with whom I consult. I hope they help you as well.

CHAPTER TWO

Dyads: The Building Blocks of a Family System

WE OFTEN hear people speak of such and such a family as being "close," or, perhaps "not close." Although people might have various interpretations of family closeness, generally they are speaking about a quality of family life. Some might define a close family as one that shares many activities and interests; others would emphasize good communication, the ability to talk out their feelings. However, true closeness is really possible only on a one-to-one basis because only in a one-to-one situation can two human beings give each other complete attention.

While the family system acts as a unit to maintain balance, the system itself is the sum of many different relationships. In fact, there are as many different relationships within each family system as there are twosomes. These twosomes are what family therapists commonly refer to as dyads. How well the family system functions as a whole depends on how well each of the one-to-one relationships is working. Each one of the twosomes in the family has the potential to become a supportive relationship or a trouble spot. Every dyad tries to strike its own balance in that twosome relationship, while each partner of the dyad tries to maintain a balance in other relationships as well.

Ideally, members of a family system make an effort to have a one-to-one relationship with all family members. Couples need to make special time when they can focus on each other, and parents need to make time to show each child special attention. As a member of a larger family system, it is also valuable to plan special time to be with parents and siblings. Even when geography keeps families apart, phone calls and letters are ways to show continued interest and affection.

The main point here is that when you are thinking about your family as a whole, and how happy you are or aren't, you need to think specifically about each person in the family and how you feel about him or her. You may find it easier to get along with one of your children than another one, you may prefer your father over your mother, and you might just as soon chat with your sister as with your spouse. However, in order for the whole to operate smoothly, each connection must work smoothly as well. And in order for a dyad to work well it has to be in balance. Each member of the dyad needs to be satisfied with the way things are.

All dyads strive to attain a balance in their twosome relationship because when the dyad is "in balance" (at rest), stress is usually lower. Thus a dyad is said to be in balance when the quality of the relationship and the roles that have been set up within the twosome are accepted, at least for the present time, by each member of the dyad. If, however, one member of the twosome is unhappy with his/her role or relationship and decides to change, the balance of the dyad is upset. Again, the term "balance" should not be understood to mean "good working order" or taken as a comment about how well the twosome works. It refers more to a state of equilibrium or rest that has been reached by the couple in which there is usually a reduction of tension, but not necessarily better functioning.

Time is, of course, an important factor in relationships. In theory, the bigger the family, the more time we would need to spend to do it right. For example, adding a second child to a family unit creates three additional dyads—new child-mother; new child-father; new child-sibling. Each of these new relationships takes away time from the existing dyads, and prospective parents often deliberate carefully before deciding to have a second child, or in deciding to have children at all. In the not so distant past, people paid less attention to this issue and having four, five, six or more children was not unusual. Today's smaller families would seem to be blessed with more time to focus on individual relationships, but they are also more likely to have two working parents and no support from the grandparent generation. This means that all our one-to-one ties must compete with our obligations to employers and not just other relationships in the family. No one can really tell you how much time is needed to keep a dyad in good working order—so much depends on the people involved and the circumstances. At one time in a marriage a couple may need to spend more time together, or one child may require more attention than the others. One thing is certain, if this is a time in life when the system is out of balance, and you or others are dissatisfied, relationships will

24

demand more time in the near future or until a new balance is found.

A key factor in how any dyad works is responsibility; and in a marital dyad, as partners in an intense emotional relationship, in running a household, and in possibly rearing children, responsibility becomes critically important. The two major areas of responsibility are functional—who does what, when, and how—and emotional. Under functional are all the household chores and the tasks of earning money and rearing children.

Ideally, couples learn to negotiate tasks in the early years of their marriage, and as new tasks arise, they have a method of dividing duties that seems fair to both. This was considerably easier when everyone agreed that he earned money, and she stayed home and cared for children. However, in the past fifteen years, the women's movement and the economy have rearranged the expectations of men and women alike. With over 40% of mothers of children under six employed, more couples than ever are sharing both areas more equally. Some agree from the start that they want a more traditional marriage, and find themselves forced to reconsider because of economics, while others may share a dream of a dual-career marriage, and place an equal priority on the work of both partners. What this means to the individual couple is that each must struggle with issues that their parents may have taken for granted.

Each of these dyads is like one of a number of building blocks stacked to make a wall. Each dyad has its own patterns of communication—a set way that the twosome operates. Remove one, or push it this way or that, and the rest must shift or fall. Relationship difficulties in families usually begin as a result of an imbalance or problem in one dyad. To work on the family system, it is necessary to figure out what goes on between each pair and how that pair affects all the other pairs.

Marital Dyad

Probably the single more important factor affecting the functioning level of the family is the quality of the marital dyad. I emphasize the marital dyad as the key building block in a family system rather than the parent-child dyad chiefly because not all couples have children. However, even in the majority of families that choose to have children, healthy family functioning proceeds best when the couple's main focus is on the marital relationship and when that relationship provides the strength to sustain the couple in their roles as parents.

Development of the marital dyad is a continuous process to be worked on, not a state to be arrived at. It begins long before anyone says, "I do!" as each person brings an experience of the workings of his or her own parents' marital relationship into the marriage. We go into marriage with knowledge of the past, and a hope of being in more control of the outcome we desire.

Well-functioning dyads usually are quite successful at maintaining balance because they see their roles and responsibilities to each other as flexible and not chiseled in granite. Life is a changing process and, over time, who earns a living and who cares for the children may fluctuate in order to provide for the continued growth of both spouses. Comments such as "I'm home first so why don't I cook and you can clean up," "I'll do the laundry if you will do the grocery shopping," and "let's both agree to clean the house together on Saturday mornings" are clear agreements to get a balance of responsibility into the dyadic relationship so that neither spouse feels overburdened.

If a spouse is unhappy in the marriage, he or she is often complaining that things are "unfair." This is a comment about uneven distribution of responsibilities. Obviously the spouse most likely to complain is the one who is feeling burdened or unloved. Statements like "I'm tired of always making the bed," "why do I always have to pay the bills," and "isn't it about time that you did something around here" are usually signs that one spouse feels the responsibilities are out of balance. The complainer is usually being overresponsible—or doing too much; and the partner is being underresponsible—or not doing enough. Unfortunately, these types of remarks are heard as an attack, and the other person usually begins to defend him/herself, and the major issues of balance and fairness never get addressed. The person doing more than his or her fair share (overresponsible) feels righteous, and the person under attack (underresponsible) feels misunderstood. The problem then escalates because they are arguing about the tip of the iceberg rather than the issue that lies below.

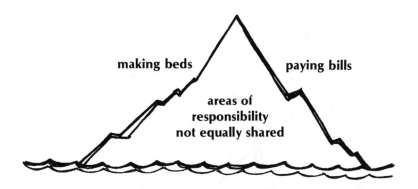

In reality it takes two people to throw a dyad out of balance, that is, one to be overresponsible and one to be underresponsible; and it takes two people to restore the balance; that is, one has to do less, and the other has to do more. Usually, the over-responsible party needs to make the first move. We consider responsibility an asset; however, being overresponsible is often a liability. In the work environment, employers reward overresponsibility by praises, raises, and promotions. The over-responsible person in the realm of human relationships, however, is usually greeted with criticism, derogatory remarks, and no appreciation because often much of his or her energy focuses on a campaign to "shape-up" the others. The overresponsible person feels the weight of responsibility for him/herself and for everyone else in the family; this style of functioning has often been learned from observing a parent function in a similar fashion (*Figure 2-1*).

The behavior of the underresponsible person is more obvious and makes him or her appear to be the one who is at fault. But blaming the underresponsible person ignores the fact that the overresponsible partner takes away the opportunity for the other to be more responsible.

Anne was 28 years old, and suffering severe depression. Her husband, Tom, was in his final year of law school, and the couple had a nine-month-old baby. Anne worked full time as a legal secretary. Although Tom helped with the baby on weekends, Anne reported that his long commute and the fact that she was breast-feeding left the majority of child-care to her. She also

Figure 2-1

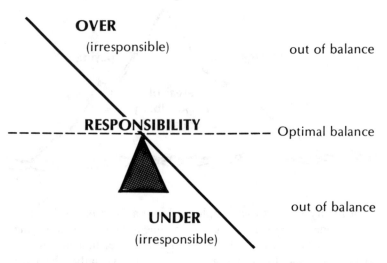

took primary responsibility for cleaning the family's five-room apartment, although she said Tom would help when asked. As the end of Tom's schooling approached, and he faced the bar examinations, she had made every effort not to disturb his study time in the evenings. She saw an important goal—establishing Tom as the main breadwinner of the family—near completion, and she didn't want to ruin anything. However, she felt constantly overtired and angry with him and the baby. She was regretting their decision to have a child, becoming dissatisfied with her job, and resenting Tom's opportunity to pursue a career. By the time she sought therapy, she was considering a divorce. She had not had sexual relations with Tom in several months, and she reported that she usually fell asleep at 9 o'clock after doing the dishes and putting the baby to bed.

It was clear that to save the relationship, the responsibilities needed to be more fairly distributed. However, when Tom came in for sessions, Anne learned that he hesitated to do things with the baby on his own because he was afraid of her criticism when he did so. He explained that when he fed the child, a job he basically enjoyed, Anne would pop her head in every few minutes to see how "things were going." She would also be the one to decide from the baby's reaction when he had had enough to eat.

Anne and Tom also discussed the housework issue. And here again, the issue seemed to be Anne's standards vs. Tom's fear of criticism. Fortunately, they were open enough to address these issues, and were able to reassign chores more equally and set aside time to enjoy life together.

This couple was fortunate. There are three reasons why this overresponsible pattern is so hard to change. First of all, the overresponsible person is cloaked in virtue. We've all heard it's better to give than to receive, and it's true to an extent; doing something for another person feels good. This good feeling can even make one feel more powerful, or indispensable to the other person. Secondly, overdoing for others distracts people from figuring out what is happening in their own lives. Most of us are constantly thinking or daydreaming during the day when we are not concentrating on a specific task. Instead of filling our daydreams with issues like "am I really happy in this job?", it can be easier to crowd the mind with details of the next thing to be done for another, or how our partner should be making this or that change. Thirdly, when someone pulls back into a merely responsible position, he or she finds out that the so-called irresponsible person functions better. This brings relief to some people, but it can also bring up huge feelings of regret. Given a choice, some of us do not choose to do things that will make us feel uncomfortable, and to recognize that efforts were misplaced can be terribly discouraging.

All dyads should strive for balanced partnerships. The degree of power or influence that each party has in a dyad is a crucial ingredient in determining its cohesiveness. In an equal relationship where power is shared, both partners have learned to give and take and to make negotiations a vital ingredient in the decision-making process; this makes both individuals feel competent and good about themselves. When power is not shared, power struggles inevitably surface in the form of competition: "I'm right—you're wrong" battles.

It may look easier to give in or not speak up in the beginning and to move toward an easier temporary solution rather than to look at the long-range effects of losing equality in the relationship. However, the balancing of power and areas of responsibility in the marital dyad are crucial factors in developing closeness in the marriage. Couples who have attained this balance have a

29

head-start in working out emotional issues (*Figure 2-2*).

Figure 2-2

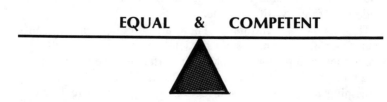

Figure 2-3 depicts some of the most common forms of imbalance in the marital dyad. As you can see, it takes two people to tip the scales. For example, no partner can be "dominant" if the other does not agree to be "submissive."

Figure 2-3

Unbalanced Marital Dyads

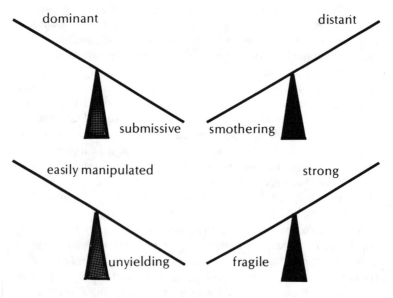

Intimacy

Up to this point in our discussion of dyads, the emphasis has been on the functional aspects of keeping the twosome going. I waited until now to do this because being able to work on the functional issues spoken of previously produces intimacy. How could someone be close to another if he or she feels used or constantly criticized? Without these areas worked out there would be underlying resentment that would lead eventually to open conflict. With a working knowledge of dyads and with an appreciation for maintaining a balanced twosome, let's take a look at what happens in the emotional sphere surrounding relationships.

Whenever one talks about emotional functioning, relationships, and dyads, the issue of closeness immediately comes to the fore. I think this occurs because of our lifelong efforts to determine how much closeness with others and how much personal space or time we need at different phases of our life. Unfortunately, we seem to have trouble maintaining the ideal degree of closeness. People often maintain so much space between themselves and others that there is hardly any feeling, or they go to the opposite extreme and get so close that they suffocate each other.

Stress tends to form when people are trying to work out the desired degree of closeness or distance that they seek in a relationship. Since the degree of closeness varies among individuals, fluctuates on certain days, and can be different at various stages of one's life, it is normal to expect the emotional environment of the dyad to be quite susceptible to upheavals. A basic assumption about emotional systems is that people seek closeness. Closeness means caring, belonging, sharing, feeling a part of, and being accepted.* Some people seek a great deal of closeness, while some seek very little. For some, a pat on the back would be a sign of real closeness, while for another only a bear hug could express it. Closeness is a fluid state rather than a permanent one; we feel more or less close at different times. People have different capacities and needs for closeness, which vary at different times.

We can visually imagine moving emotionally close to—or away from—people. When one person moves toward another person, he or she increasingly contacts the emotional core of the other person.

*Thomas F. Fogarty, "The Distancer and the Pursuer," *The Family* (1979), vol. 7, no. 1, p. 11.

This can be touchy ground, and the temptation to pull back, to divert one's energies and attention to someone or something else can be quite strong at times like this for both parties. For example, most of us can remember changing the topic of conversation, or talking about a third person, or inviting another person to join the twosome in order to lower the intensity of the relationship. Sometimes one is aware of this process and sometimes one is not. These are examples of lowering the intensity of the dyad in order to protect or gain personal space.

Figure 2-4

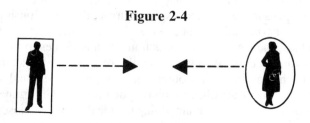

As people move toward each other (*Figure 2-4*), the emotional intensity in the dyad builds. This is true in all significant relationships. Both partners in a dyad have to decide how much closeness they need in order for a given relationship to be satisfying for them. This is not an easy process; seeking the amount of closeness we desire is a lifelong process of moving closer, experiencing how that feels, and then backing away some, deciding how that feels, and then moving again—always hoping for that perfect degree of closeness, connectedness, and sense of completion. That state is seldom reached for very long, but rather is a goal that we continually seek. People strive for this sense of completion and closeness in different ways. Some are in a great rush; others do not seem to care at all. Some run while others walk. Some of us think closeness is reached by endless talking, while others believe it is arrived at in silence.

Closeness and Fusion

When striving for closeness, the intensity of the feelings can lead to a state where one or both people feel overwhelmed by the relationship. This experience can feel as though one has lost one's sense of self. This "too-close" state is called fusion, and it causes people to distance in a relationship, almost as a necessity for survival.

This fused state is actually quite common in marriage. For example, a couple may experience very close times; these intimate times happen when both parties focus on the relationship, and are able to find joy in shared feelings and experiences. However, what often happens is that one partner comes home looking for this kind of experience to bolster an ego defeated by a bad day at the office. The unspoken need is "love me enough so that what happened today doesn't matter." If the partner is also out of sorts, or just plain busy, he or she may not hear the other's distress. This piles disappointment on top of all the other bad feelings. Things can get worse if both parties are under a good deal of stress, as frequently happens in marital dyads. Each may rely more on the other to calm anxiety; and when this need is not met, each may lose the all-important sense of self. This is a frightening feeling that creates more anxiety, and may make one of the parties feel smothered. A natural reaction to this feeling of being smothered (fusion) is to instigate a fight (sometimes over nothing), in order to gain the distance or breathing room that he or she needs.

Figure 2-5

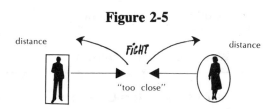

In attempting to arrive at the desired degree of closeness in a dyad, movement comes from both partners. Ironically, major events usually result in movement from both; however, not to the same degree or in the same direction. Take for example the chart on page 34 (*Figure 2-6*), which depicts the movement of a hypothetical couple around numerous events and issues in a 25-year marriage. The direction of the arrows indicates movement toward or away from each other, and the length of each arrow represents the intensity. For example, at the time of engagement and marriage, both were moving toward each other, but the husband was more interested in seeking closeness than was his wife.

Figure 2-6

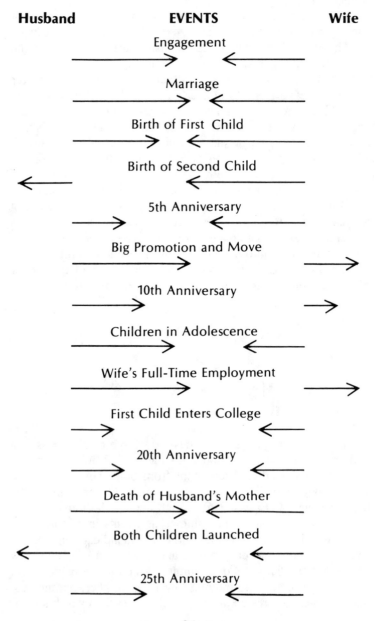

Husband	EVENTS	Wife

Engagement

Marriage

Birth of First Child

Birth of Second Child

5th Anniversary

Big Promotion and Move

10th Anniversary

Children in Adolescence

Wife's Full-Time Employment

First Child Enters College

20th Anniversary

Death of Husband's Mother

Both Children Launched

25th Anniversary

By the time of their fifth anniversary, the wife was moving toward her husband, desiring more closeness, while he was seeking more personal space and moving toward his career goals. When she took a full-time job, she began to move outside the dyad to have some of her needs met, and he began to move toward her. This movement continued as the couple faced other life-cycle events—the marriage of children and the death of parents.

Distancing and Pursuing

Dr. Tom Fogarty originated use of the terms *pursuing* and *distancing* to describe the two styles of emotional interaction which people tend to use while trying to work out the desired degree of closeness they seek in their one-to-one relationship. Basically, people who tend to use distancing as their style of emotional interaction are looking for space, more alone time, and are less likely to talk about feelings in their relationships. Pursuers, on the other hand, seek more closeness, more together time, and are eager to share feelings in their relationships. These styles can be considered in terms of a continuum, as shown in Figure 2-7.

Figure 2-7

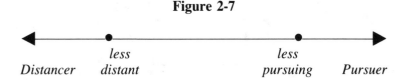

| Distancer | *less* distant | | *less* pursuing | Pursuer |

However, one cannot think of a person as a pure "distancer" or a pure "pursuer." Rather, each person is a mixture of both styles. Under stress, a person will most likely lean in one direction or the other; but people change their styles of emotional interaction around different issues and at different points in their life. For example, in the graph of the imaginary marriage, each partner changed direction more than once. There can be no value judgment placed on either distancing or pursuing; each is simply a style of interacting, and neither is right or wrong.

It is interesting to note that most marital relationships contain someone who tends to be a distancer and someone who tends to be a pursuer. Opposites attract. You may be wondering: can you have two pursuers or two distancers in a marital relationship? Anything is possible, but generally, it doesn't seem to happen that way. Two distancers would be so far apart that there would be insufficient contact to hold the twosome together (*Figure 2-8*), and two pursuers would probably burn each other out in no time (*Figure 2-9*).

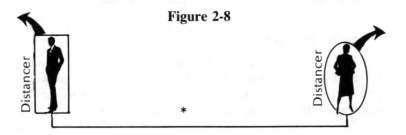

Figure 2-8

Figure 2-9

There is no strict sex-stereotyping regarding distancers and pursuers. Rather, one's style of relating to others is more a factor of the types of emotional relationships that one experiences within one's family of origin. However, since women have for centuries been the emotional centers of the family while men have been expected to leave the family in order to make a living, there is still a strong tendency for women to be more pursuing and for men to lean toward distancing.

The characteristics listed in Figure 2-10 are general tendencies only of each style, and change around different issues.

---

*The symbol ⌐_____⌐ is used by family therapists to indicate that a man, represented by a square ☐, and a woman, represented by a circle ○, are married.

Figure 2-10
"P" AND "D" CHART

PURSUERS	*with regard to*	DISTANCERS

"timing"

—*now* is the best time to do it, especially if there is a problem to be solved or some upset or anxiety to be discussed.	—*later* is the best time to do it, what's the rush, there's always tomorrow; with regard to upsets and problems, they are better left alone at first, calm is more important, peace at all cost.

"problems" or "upsets"

—should be thoroughly talked out as soon as possible with a significant other.	—should be handled alone, privately, by yourself.
—would prefer not to go to bed angry or upset, and would definitely want to avoid periods of not talking to each other.	—would prefer silence and a "cooling-off" period—even if it takes a long time.

"when fighting"

—would like to make up in the shortest possible time.	—would prefer a slower and longer making-up period.

"movement"—especially under stress

—would move toward people.	—would move toward objects.
—would move away from objects.	—would move away from people.
—absence feels lonely and empty.	—"absence makes the heart grow fonder," people not appreciated until they are gone.

"changes"

—more anxious for change, but usually defines change as the other person changing rather than self change.	—less anxious for change and if it happens, sees it as a slow, evolving process.

"therapy" or "counseling"

—usually the initiator, wants to solve things	—usually doesn't see the need for counseling or even the problem, sometimes accompanies the other to therapy to keep peace, sometimes refuses.

Figure 2-11
OTHER GENERAL DESCRIPTORS

PURSUERS	*DISTANCERS*
—take a more active role.	—tend to be more passive and to look at things from a distance.
	—are protective of space and privacy, will withdraw into their own space to consider personal or life problems.
—see the future in terms of being connected to others.	—can be counted on for concrete help—like helping get a car started on a cold morning—but not for a strong sense of emotional connectedness.
—are hopeful, generally, when pondering the future.	—are generally less optimistic.
—are more interested in sharing feelings and anxieties.	—are more interested in sharing facts or information.
	—are more likely to feel intruded upon or suffocated.
—tend to be overresponsible regarding the emotions of others.	—are more focused on what is happening in their heads.
—will turn to another person when frustrated.	—will turn to self for direction when frustrated.

—tend to be doers, more active, and at times will try to precipitate a reaction from the distancer whom they are pursuing.	—are more in control and logical.
—are more outgoing.	—are more dificult to get to know.
—seek completion or fulfillment in the companionship of others.	—find completion or fulfillment difficult, so don't risk being vulnerable with others.
	—tend to assume a pursuing posture around the issues of sex and anger.
	—avoid feelings because they produce anxiety.

When people are seeking or avoiding closeness in a relationship, their movements can be described as a "two-step."* Some twosomes get locked into this "two-step" and stay there. The pursuer blames the distancer for never being available, for being too involved with objects outside the relationship (golf, work, etc.), for not caring enough, for being too cold and logical or for not measuring up to expectations. The distancer then responds with a litany of: "what a nag, never satisfied, always on my case, never leaves me alone, can't even breathe around here anymore."

Let's look at an example that shows the dynamic movement in this process. Adam and Barbara have been married for twenty years and have a 17-year-old daughter named Gill. Adam has always been a workaholic, but since starting his own business five years ago, he has spent even more time away from the family. As Adam moved toward his business, Barbara became increasingly lonely. She allowed Gill to meet many of her emotional needs through an over-involved (parent-child) relationship with her. At 17, Gill is applying to a college in another state. This

---

*Fogarty, op. cit., p. 13; referred to as the "Bowen two-step."

throws the family into emotional upheaval because it upsets the balance of the dyads.

Adam at this stage is tending toward a distancer-style of inter-action; he has moved away from his wife toward an object, his business. Barbara, on the other hand, has moved toward a person (outside of herself) to help her meet her emotional needs. Thus, Barbara tends to be a pursuer. I would conjecture that Adam and Barbara's "two-step" went something like what is shown in Figure 2-12 until Barbara became exhausted pursuing and moved toward her daughter to get some balance and some of her emotional needs met.

Figure 2-12

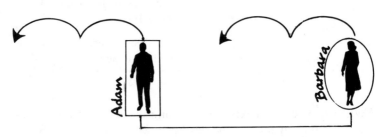

Originally, Barbara probably looked to Adam to meet her emotional needs, so in the early days of their marriage she probably pursued him. She would take two steps toward Adam, hoping he would meet her need for closeness. However, Adam was sensitive to emotional intensity and uncomfortable with that degree of closeness, so he took two steps away from his wife. They still remained together (connected), but at a fixed distance from each other. Likewise, when Adam's pursuit surfaced, usually in the form of sexual advances, Barbara would do her "two-step" and distance from him.

In terms of dyads, Adam and Barbara's relationship is an example of how neither spouse was successful at having his or her emotional needs met within the marital relationship. Instead of developing closeness and intimacy, they both chose to move toward something else that would allow them to avoid facing their lack of connectedness. This approach only puts the issue of intimacy temporarily on the back burner. It will surface again, as it does when Gill tries to leave for college; the additional problem now is that the pattern of avoiding intimacy by using child and job has had five years to develop.

What Is the Problem with Pursuing and Distancing?

The problem is that both pursuers and distancers contribute to maintaining a constant space or fixed distance between themselves and the other person (*Figure 2-13*).

Figure 2-13

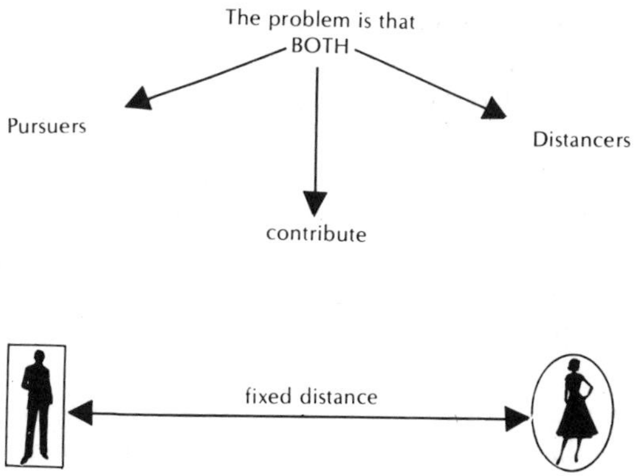

Parent-Child Dyad

During the last several decades, the parent-child relationship has received tremendous attention and focus, both in the media and in the psychological literature. The main function of the parent-child relationship in this country during the last century has been to encourage the independence of the child; this is quite different from earlier years, when the child was seen as a vital contributor to the family economy, who seldom moved far from his or her birthplace. This shift in focus has had significant effects on the workings of the parent-child dyad. Before the industrial revolution, the child was seen not only as contributing to the economy of the family, but also as the future mainstay of the family—both socially and economically. The emphasis was to raise children who would stay around home, make a contribution, bring along the next generation, and in due course take care of the older generation. After the Industrial Revolution, there began to be a need to raise children who were capable of leaving home to go and find work outside the family. This change has led to one of the family's most important developmental tasks, that is, to encourage its members to become self-sufficient, while at the same time staying emotionally connected. Here again, it is a question of maintaining balance.

This issue, often referred to as the ability to separate, is one issue that we all struggle with from the time we leave the womb until the moment we reach the tomb. Separation can be viewed as a lifelong process that everyone experiences, of becoming independent from the people to whom we are most emotionally connected. Being "separate" does not mean being emotionally cut off from loved ones. Rather it means that one connects to loved ones in a way that allows for mutual freedom of choice.

The separation issue begins at birth when the baby leaves the mother's womb. Both must separate—the baby must adapt to the new environment, and the mother must adjust to no longer having the baby inside her. The separation process continues through the next months, and goes through a dramatic phase when the baby begins literally to move away from mother and learns to walk. The child needs to learn that movement away from mother is good and that he or she will still be loved when he or she returns. Here we see that, before the age of 2 years, the groundwork is set for the ultimate goal of parenthood and healthy family functioning: namely, that the child will be able to leave as an independent, functioning person, and that the parents will be able to let him or her go. There are many testing points along the way which can be used as indicators to see how the child and the parents are accomplishing their mutual goal of separation. For example, how will the parents and the child react when the child enters school, how will they handle the options of camp and overnight visits with friends, and how will they negotiate the many other comings and goings of family life?

Families teach autonomy to their children not so much by what they say but by the way they interact with each other. If parents give the impression to a young child that the world is generally a safe place to live and that people can be trusted, the child will learn these attitudes and find it easier to move away

42

from the immediate family and reach out to others to make friends.

Saying we want our children to be successful adults is admittedly easier than getting them there. The task is always a constantly changing one of finding the right functional and emotional balance for the child's age and stage. How much we do for a child and how much we expect a child to do for him/herself and for the system varies according to the child's age. And while our emotional attachment to our children is always strong, loving them means being willing to move over as their friends and, eventually, a spouse and their own children become more important in their daily lives.

As in marriage, responsibility is a key issue; and trouble often surfaces in the form of one overresponsible party and one underresponsible party. This is not to blame the child in question, or to slap the wrist of the mother or father. What is needed is to look at the relationship and identify who is the overresponsible one and who is the underresponsible one, and to talk about how the imbalance occurred. If the parent is overresponsible, then he or she may see the child as "lazy" or "selfish." If the child is feeling overresponsible, he or she may be having the immediate payoff of feeling very necessary at home, but be having difficulty making friends or, in adolescence, planning to leave. The imbalance is a two-way street that results out of the emotional needs of both the parent and the child. Children from the first day of life display different personality traits. One child in the family may fight responsibility tooth and nail, and lead a mother to do everything just to keep the peace, while another may try to imitate her and take on too much responsibility for his or her own age. Children also are extremely sensitive to gaps in the marital dyad. In order to feel more important than "Mommy" or "Daddy," a child will often try to fill a role in the other parent's life. Thus, a mother and daughter may become "best friends," and the mother may share more thoughts and feelings with a daughter than with her husband. The problem comes when the daughter wants to leave. Parents understandably experience loss when a child leaves home, but when an overresponsible child leaves, the loss is even greater. Feelings of guilt and genuine concern for the parent may prevent such a child from leaving home at all. Children also have different emotional styles, just like adults—one may go to her room and hibernate, while another wraps himself around your ankle and whines. How you view either reaction, and whether or not you label it a problem, depends on your own emotional style and attitudes about parenting.

Whatever the original source of the problem, a family working on a problem with one child needs to look at all other relationships—particularly the marriage—at the same time. If one child is able to provoke so much upset in the home, then all the other relationships are out of balance as well.

When looking at trouble spots in a parent-child dyad, the task is to see whether they exist independently of problems in the marital dyad. They rarely do, but sometimes difficulties in the marriage are a result of a difficult parent-child relationship, and sometimes a difficult parent-child relationship is the result of marital difficulties. In the first case, a mother who had no problem adjusting to a first child may find herself with a second child whose personality is at odds with her own. Or a father who had no trouble getting along with his daughter may have problems with his son. A child's chronic illness or a learning disability may also cause imbalance. In such cases, the genuine difficulties of parenting may drain so much energy from the parents that the marriage ultimately suffers as well.

It is often harder for parents to see that the opposite is true, that a weakness in their marriage has led to problems with a child. This too is understandable, because addressing problems in the marriage can be much more threatening to the family as a whole. In an effort to protect the marriage and the family system and avoid permanent disruption, both parties may ignore issues they secretly believe could divide them.

Since families often come to treatment when a child is acting up, or having difficulty breaking away in later adolescence, this may be the first time you are seriously looking at the way your marriage works. It is important not to waste energy on blaming yourself or your spouse, and focus positive efforts on finding out how this problem with your child has helped you get along until now.

The Walker family was referred by school officials for therapy because of difficulties that the oldest boy Bill was having at school. Mrs. Walker made the initial phone contact to set up an appointment and was quite concerned and baffled by her son's recent tailspin. She reported that Bill had been a very responsible son and, until recently, had done quite well in school. Mrs. Walker was articulate, cared about her son's well-being, and was anxious to get the problems resolved. When I asked her how Bill's father viewed his son's present predicament, she said, "Of course he cares, but he has had a drinking problem for the last several years and probably would not be much help at this time." My initial approach was to see how the dyads in this family operated, to explore areas of responsibility, and to see if the issue of alcohol had clouded the family's attempt to establish a workable balance.

Bill is 17 years old, the oldest son of John and Ruth Walker. The Walkers have two other children: Mike, 14, and Sally, 12. Bill is in his senior year of high school, has been a solid B student, a leading member of the school government and senior class activities, a highly respected young man both by his teachers and fellow students, and an active member in his church group. Early in the second semester of his senior year Bill's parents were notified that he had not completed any of his college applications, that he was failing a required course for graduation, and that he had been cutting classes.

Let's take a look at how the dyads work in the Walker family.

Marital Dyad. John and Ruth have been married for 20 years; the last two years have been filled with struggles over John's excessive drinking. The couple separated once and Ruth allowed John to return without noticeable improvement in his sobriety because "the children needed their father at home." Their style of fighting is to yell and scream at each other and, although it never gets physical, the children are often caught in the middle and wind up taking sides.

Parent–Child Dyads. *Mother–Bill:* Mrs. Walker is an independent woman who tries to make do on her own resources while trying to conceal her husband's drinking problem from the community. Basically, because Bill has been a good, responsible young man, she has unwittingly allowed him to do more than what is appropriate for his age. The boundaries between parent and child have become blurred and she would treat him at times as an adult and an equal. When decisions needed to be made regarding the house, finances, and the other children, she looked to Bill for his opinion. When she was feeling lonely, she often leaned on him for support. Mrs. Walker was trying to balance

45

out what she was missing in the marital dyad by having a supportive relationship with her son. She is not a bad woman; she cares deeply for her family. Although she will miss her son greatly, she wants Bill to go away to college to be free of "this mess" and to develop on his own. However, the message hasn't been clearly perceived by Bill, who has assumed an overresponsible role.

Bill also played a part in this skewed relationship with his mother. He liked taking on additional responsibility and having a special place with her, but he felt guilty about taking over his father's role. Bill has taken on an adult role very early and when he falters in his senior year his mother finds it very hard to respond to him as a 17-year-old rather than as a grown man.

Father–Bill: Bill is angry with his father for the drinking. He tried in the beginning to get him to stop but now he pretty much ignores him. Occasionally, he finds himself in the role of being a father to his father because when his father drinks he comes to Bill for guidance and approval.

Bill–Sibling Dyads: Although Bill is often a good older brother, he occasionally has stormy fights with Mike and Sally. It is a very touchy situation when a sibling crosses the parental boundary line and becomes the disciplinarian. This became very clear one night when Mike returned home drunk from a party and he became nasty to his mother. Instead of Mrs. Walker calling Mike's father to help her deal with the situation, she woke up Bill. Mr. Walker was home but he already was in bed and drunk. Bill also found himself in the role of trying to give support and guidance to his siblings about getting good grades in school and staying out of truble.

The dyadic relationships and structure in the Walker family are tipped out of balance. It is not surprising to see stress pass from one dyad to another and, therefore, for a symptom to appear. It shows up this time in Bill because he is the one most vulnerable to the upcoming shift in the family should he graduate and leave for college. It might be easier if Bill did not graduate and, therefore, the existing precarious balance in the Walker family would not have to change.

Bill gave plenty of excuses for failing American History, for not completing his college applications, and for skipping classes. However, he was not aware that he was having trouble deciding about leaving home in the fall. How would the family do without him? Who would support his mother? Who would look out for his younger sibs? Would his father drink more if he wasn't there? What would happen if Mike acted up? Leaving home for all adolescents is a major developmental task, and it is normal and predictable that some will have trouble with it. Bill's leaving home significantly changes all the dyads in the family and can become that much more difficult when his role has stabilized the family's stress and balanced the dyads. The failing grade, cutting classes, and lack of college applications were just signs that Bill was having a difficult time thinking about moving on. It is important in cases like this to focus on the real issue rather than to get caught up in the symptoms. Let's also remember that when the structure of a family system becomes imbalanced, several of the dyads must be under stress. When you take a look at these dyads, you find out that the dyad would not be as skewed as it is if both members of the twosome were not contributing to the process. Just as it takes two people to make a relationship function well, it takes two to offset the equilibrium and keep it that way. Mr. Walker, Mrs. Walker, and Bill all played a part in this process. An awareness that one is part of the problem and, therefore, part of the solution is a good starting point for making some changes in one's life.

Pursuers and Distancers in Parent–Child Relationships

Styles of distancing and pursuing also apply to interactions between parents and children. I have been focusing on couple or marital relationships but, before concluding, it is important to say a word about how these styles affect the parent-child dyad. I will only take a look at two of the most common examples—the pursuing mother and the distant father.

Pursuing Mothers. Some mothers pursue their children to fill up something that is incomplete in their own lives and then find it very difficult to pull back. Most often their pursuit attempts to "shape up" the child, with the typical result of driving the child further away. They find it hard to alter their pursuit, fearing that the child would only be worse if they were to back off.

Sometimes mothers become exhausted with attempts to "shape up" a child. They then back off in a very angry and distant way. They have given up; they're totally frustrated. This usually doesn't work any better and the involvement is still there in the angry feelings.

Distant Fathers. Men have been socialized for a long time to leave the emotional needs of their children to their wives. By doing this, men have been missing out on a beautiful opportunity to know their children. Distant fathers can care very much about their children; they just express it in a distant style—like working 16-hour days, which makes them good providers but often too tired to handle the relationship needs of their children.

Here again the issue of balance must be dealt with. Is father working because it is a matter of meat and potatoes for his family or is he working and absent from the family because it fits his style of interaction better? Likewise, a husband/father may need some recreation on the golf course, but there is a balance between not playing at all and playing every Saturday and Sunday!

A pursuing mother and a distancing father often find themselves in the same household; and the combination can add up to trouble for all concerned. What frequently happens is that through these basic differences in emotional style, a permanent imbalance gets set up in the family system. A father may permanently distance himself from his wife and children, and seek refuge in his job or outside activities, while the mother may use her children to fill up the gap left by the lack of closeness with her husband, and her lack of focus on her own growth (*Figure 2-14*). This leads us naturally into the concept of triangles, the topic of Chapter 3.

Figure 2-14

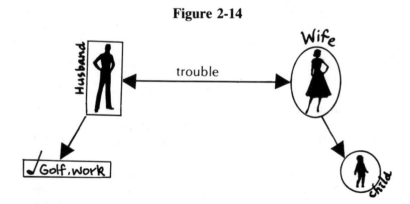

48

Sibling–Sibling Dyads

One final word before moving on to triangles. Any of you who have more than one child, or who have grown up with siblings, are aware of the tension that can be caused in a family by fights among children. Frequently fights result from one or another thinking that something isn't fair. Kids fighting in the back seat can ruin the nicest family outing, planned by the most well-meaning parents, but wise parents will stay clear. Some complaints of things not being fair may need parental attention, but probably, unless the danger of physical harm is present, it is better to let the siblings work it out themselves. If children are of different ages, parents need to be firm in explaining to each that the privileges and duties apply to age. Squabbling is still inevitable, but parents can at least endure with a clear conscience if they know they have carefully thought through how each child is treated by the both of them.

References

Thomas F. Fogarty, "The Distancer and the Pursuer," *The Family* (1979), vol. 7, no. 1.

Jerry M. Lewis, *How's Your Family?* (New York: Brunner/Mazel, 1979).

Walter Toman, *Family Constellation* (New York: Springer, 1977).

CHAPTER THREE

Triads: Building Blocks for Relationship Problems

WHEN PEOPLE have trouble working out the balance in their one-to-one relationships, they often bring in another person to offset the emotional upset generated by the imbalance. By "bring in," I mean they literally ask someone else to support their side. They bring someone else into the conversation so the topic gets less personal (thus less intense) or they change the topic, again to move away from the emotionally charged subject. It is normal at times for relationships to upset us; however, the two people involved have the option of dealing directly with the stress between them—which is what is recommended here—or involving a third person to try to calm down the anxieties, insecurities, and stresses that intense relationships bring. Problems in communication occur when two people include a third person in their one-to-one relationship because their twosome is lacking in some way. This process of building triads—"communicating in triangles"— attempts to stabilize one-to-one relationships, but prevents any hope of direct communication.

The concept of triangles is a basic tenet of the family-systems approach to emotional functioning.* Triangles occur in all families and in all relationships, tending to surface when the emotional atmosphere is intense. Two people attempt to defuse their relationship with a third person (or object). That might sound like a good idea at first. Why not calm down the intensity? Well, the difficulty with triangles is that the real issue is not being dealt with; it has simply been pushed aside. And since triangles tend to repeat themselves, no progress will be made toward solving the real communication problem. Triangles avoid a problem rather than face the real issue directly.

The number of opportunities for triangles to form is very high because the potential for this process to occur happens every time a third person is added in some way to the dyad. For example, a normal and frequent occurrence experienced by many new

*Murray Bowen, *Family Theory in Clinical Practice*, New York: Jason Aronson, 1978.

families is a shift in the marital dyad at the birth of a new child as couples often need to do some restructuring and balancing of roles, responsibilities, and time allotments. Ideally, this predictable shift is only temporary.

Most of us get into triangles; they are difficult to stay out of completely because it is hard to always deal directly with another person in a dyad on all issues. I am not condoning triangles, just acknowledging their natural frequency. We, therefore, should not be surprised to discover ourselves triangling a third person into our communications system. Unfortunately, triangles prevent closeness, create distance, cloud real issues, and temporarily cool off a problem without effecting any real change. It might be appropriate to be in a triangle with an acquaintance at the office because we do not seek closeness with everyone we meet, but in marriage and with other family members, relying on triangles is a risky choice.

Triangles form out of emotional reactions to major events within the family system. Sometimes they occur because the couple has fused, and when they see a difference it frightens them, so they look for a way to get rid of tension as quickly as possible. Other times, there may be a very weak connection that requires each partner to seek satisfaction in other relationships. Triangles may be present early in the marriage as the couple first tries to negotiate closeness with each other, and break away from their families of origin. This explains why one of the most common triangles in a marriage involves an in-law and the spouse.

Am I in a Triangle?

People are often unaware that they are caught in a triangle. They know that something is not right but they cannot figure out what it is. If you feel yourself pulling in a third person to calm down an emotional issue between yourself and someone else, you are probably caught in a triangle. Likewise, if you feel that you have been pulled into a one-to-one relationship in order to defuse it, you are probably again caught in a triangle.

Another way by which you might recognize that triangles exist within the family would be to observe the sides family members take when there is an emotional struggle. If you and someone you care about are in a triangle with someone, or something, he or she (or it) may be the topic of much conversation between you. When a triangle exists, such conversations could constantly be just short of an argument. You and your spouse might take opposite sides on an issue, and find yourselves returning again and again to the topic with every new development in the relationship system. The issue could also become an unmentionable (this is how family secrets start), something or someone that is never brought up by either of you because you fear the consequences. Or, as we saw in Chapter 2, it could represent a cause for the pursuer, and a constant annoyance to the distancer.

You might also know that you are in a triangle if you recognize the pull and intensity of a closed system. Triangles thrive in the emotional atmosphere of a closed system. When a system is closed, people are not free to change their emotional position (closeness or distance) in relation to other members in the system without someone else feeling hurt by it. Movement toward or away from people is acutely felt in a closed system because those in it perceive that there is only a finite amount of closeness to be shared. The total possibility for closeness is perceived to be a fixed quantity; movement by A toward B is seen by C as taking away some of the closeness that C had with A (*Figure 3-1*).

Figure 3-1

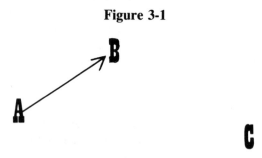

People operating in a closed system view each other as in competition for a finite amount of love. In an open system they accept that relationships have a natural rhythm—over time we move closer and then further away—without losing affection and acceptance. However, a truly open system requires a certain amount of self-contentment on the part of all members, which is difficult to achieve at all times. Stress can prompt a relationship system which was open—where responsibilities, power, and feelings were shared equally—to move in the direction of being closed. For example, if a dual-career couple has a child, and the wife decides to take a break from her career, she may find herself cut off from friends and the self-esteem she found in her work. Jealousy of the husband's continued connection to the outside world could develop to the detriment of the marital relationship. In order to prevent the relationship from becoming closed, the wife would have to face her ambivalence about motherhood, or her feelings of loss about her career, and make her own separate peace with these issues. Then, as a couple they would need to talk out the future so that competition for a limited amount of connectedness did not become the prevalent pattern of the marriage. So if you feel that your movement toward or away from one person in a system upsets a third person, you may well be in a closed system.

Not Always People/Not Every Three

Before going on, I would like to discuss two additional concepts about triangles. Up to this point in our discussion, triangles have involved three people. It is important to point out that not every group of three people is a triangle. Three people having coffee and talking about the new boss need not be in a triangle. In order for the process of triangling to occur, there must be a close and intense relationship between two people and an emotional issue that leads one, or both, to seek a third person as an ally.

The other point I would like to add to our notion of triangles is that the third party of the triangle need not be another person—it can be an object, an issue, or an event. It really does not matter what the third party is, as long as it serves to disguise the real issue and avoid change.

Let's take a look at a very normal and familiar situation in which a potential triangle could occur in which the third part is not a person, but rather, is a job promotion. Larry and Rose have been married for two years and Larry has just received a super promotion. For the next several months, Larry's energy and movement are toward the new job with its added demands and exciting challenges. He is more focused on work and less on Rose. This

53

is a natural happening, common to all of us; the important thing to watch for is how the marital dyad balances out several months after the shift has occurred. Hopefully, as Larry adjusts to his new job, he will again move toward his wife and have the job in perspective. However, if they are unable to reestablish a balance, the triangle depicted in Figure 3-2 would illustrate Larry's movement away from Rose and leave one to wonder what direction Rose would take to achieve balance for herself. Would she pursue Larry for more closeness, might she suggest that it's time to start a family, or would she get closer to other family members, such as her mother? Other common examples when the third part of the triangle is not a person are: a drinking problem, a drug problem, an affair, the TV set, a football game, or the women's movement.

Figure 3-2

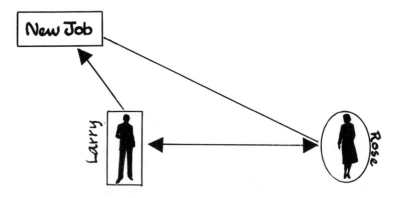

The triangle serves the purpose intended admirably—for a time. It balances the trouble with the dyad. Each party can avoid the real issue by involving a third party to meet his or her needs, or each may find a superficial closeness in joining together to fight the third member of the triangle. For example, a young couple may move far away to avoid dealing with their families of origin; but cutting off from "them" means that the couple has not truly solved the problem of separating. Each merely brings in someone else—the new spouse—to put distance between him or her and the respective parents. Later, such a couple would be vulnerable to other triangles which may not work so well (e.g., an affair) because that is how they have learned to solve difficulties in an intense relationship.

Triangles Proliferate

When a family system gets out of balance, a triangle usually forms. In many situations, however, there is not just one triangle but several that interlock. This occurs because if a dyad is stressed and the members move away from the dyad to attempt to resolve the problem, both of them could choose another person or object to try to stabilize the relationship. Let's return to our example of Adam, Barbara, and Gill from Chapter 2, in which there are several active triangles in progress. Adam has been a workaholic spending much time away from his wife and daughter; Barbara moved toward her daughter as Adam moved toward his business and allowed Gill to fill many of her closeness needs. At 17, Gill is applying for college in another state, and this throws the family into emotional upheaval.

Figure 3-3

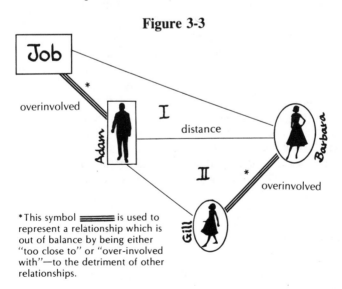

*This symbol ===== is used to represent a relationship which is out of balance by being either "too close to" or "over-involved with"—to the detriment of other relationships.

One could predict that Gill's movement toward college and autonomy would upset the emotional balance in this closed system. The forecast would be that members of this system would not be free to change their emotional position vis-à-vis each other because they believe that there is only a limited amount of closeness available; therefore, if someone is to leave home, someone else will end up feeling deprived.

In terms of triangles, Adam and Barbara's relationship is an example of how neither spouse was successful at having emotional needs met within the marital relationship. Instead of developing closeness and intimacy they both chose to triangle in something else that would allow them to avoid facing their lack of connectedness.

This environment is conducive for Gill to become symptomatic and develop a problem that would keep her from moving on to college. Her inability to move on would stabilize her parents' relationship even though they would be very upset about her failure to move on and probably not realize what was contributing to it.

Adam and Barbara chose to triangle in third parties that were socially acceptable—a job and a child—but at great cost to their marital relationship and their daughter. Figure 3-3 signifies how Adam chose to deal with closeness by triangling toward a job (**I**) and how Barbara, in the absence of her husband, chose to allow her daughter to meet many of her emotional and companionship needs (**II**). This is an example of interlocking triangles attempting to resolve an imbalance in the marital dyad; they did accomplish some calm as well as establish a fixed distance between the couple. (It is important to point out here that Barbara is not deliberately sacrificing her daughter. On the contrary, Barbara's original movement toward her daughter was probably quite well intentioned. She had no idea it would become such an emotional crutch to her as her husband continued his movement toward his business.)

Collaboration

Before describing some specific triangles, I would like to say a word about collaboration. Collaboration means that everyone in a triangle must agree to the set-up, or there's no triangle. Obviously, a child's collaboration is easily won because he or she lacks maturity to see potential problems. Children exist for the moment and think in terms of immediate goals, and they rarely need coaxing if they see a reward around the corner. If a child joins a triangle with the parents, he or she can count on increased attention from one or both parents, which is its own reward.

In triangles with three adults, each has a stake in joining, although it may be harder to admit what it is. Generally, the reward is taking attention off some real issue, and avoiding the need to face the change process. Each person feels safer in the triangle than in starting a shake-up of the family system. Unfortunately, shake-ups are as inevitable as change in the weather. Sooner or later an outside event (e.g., a change at work, or in the national economy), or an internal event (e.g., a birth, or the death of a family member) forces everyone to shift. However, when a triangle shifts, the frustration felt by all parties saps energy from dealing with the real problem at hand. Everyone wastes a lot of time getting nowhere except to temporarily blow away the smoke. Since the fire is still there, they soon find the smoke has returned.

Since there is only a fixed amount of closeness available in a closed system, no one wants to give up the limited intimacy and connectedness that he or she has. That is why it is so hard for people to make changes. The degree of closeness they experience, they know; and they are afraid to risk losing it by attempting change. The new experience which could possibly be brought about by positive change would be a new and unfamiliar experience. All change, whether positive or negative, causes some stress and anxiety. Everyone in the system collaborates to maintain the system's status quo, even if the status quo is uncomfortable for all concerned.

Degree of Stress and the Triangling Process

Let's examine how crucial the degree of anxiety or stress is in determining the triangling process.

Figure 3-4 (next page) represents a closed system, a communication pattern that brings the son in to defuse many issues in the marriage. In this case, let's assume the mother turns to her son for some of the closeness she misses in the marriage.

The lines in Figure 3-4 are of equal length because the system is not under stress; that is, although the one-to-one relationships

Figure 3-4

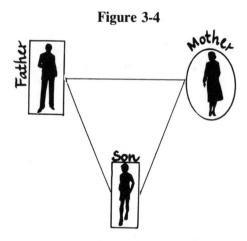

are not working at optimal level, they are, nevertheless, calm. There is not enough anxiety present at this moment in the system to stress either the marital dyad or the parent–child dyad enough to upset the balance and move one person closer to another. Figure 3-5 represents one possible shift that might occur when the stress of Dad losing his job hits the system.

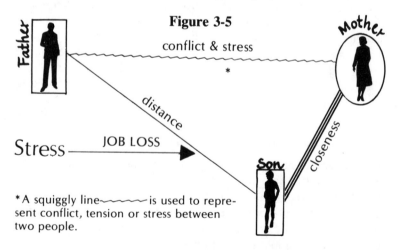

Figure 3-5

conflict & stress

*

distance

Stress —— JOB LOSS ➤

closeness

*A squiggly line〜〜〜is used to represent conflict, tension or stress between two people.

This is only one possibility. It appears that when the husband lost his job, he began to fight more with his wife. The son then moved away from his one-to-one relationship with his father into an overresponsible and protective relationship with his mother. Much more information would be needed in order to discuss this example adequately. This example is meant to show in a simple way how the degree of stress exacerbates the triangling process.

More People/More Possible Triangles

One last point needs to be made before looking at several different types of triangles. The more people in a family (*Figure 3-6*), the greater the number of potential triangles.

Figure 3-6

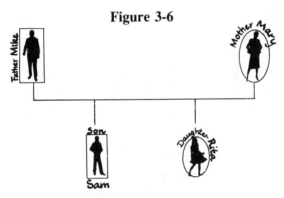

Figure 3-7 (page 60) shows a few of the triangular possibilities that the family of four in Figure 3-6 could get into as they work out their issues of closeness and intimacy.

Various Types of Triangles

Up until now, I have been discussing how common and frequent it is for triangles to form in families because of the potential for closeness that exists in those relationships. The potential for triangles occurs whenever a third person or issue is added to a dyad, as in the cases of a new baby and a job promotion. It does not have to happen, but the possibility is present unless the dyad can reestablish a balance. Remembering that triangles hinder closeness and try to calm down an emotional situation without addressing the real issues, let's take a look at a few examples of

Figure 3-7

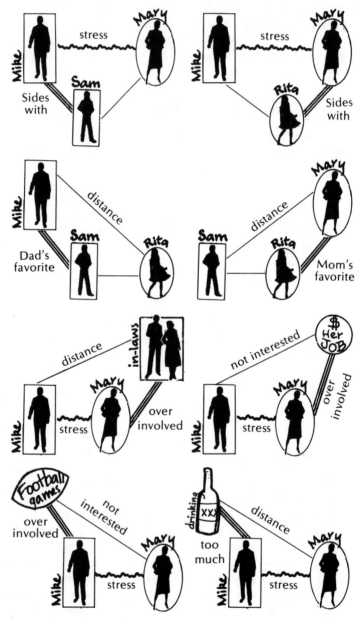

the more problematic triangles that disrupt marital and family relationships.

1. In-law Triangles. These types of triangles are most common in the early years of marriage, but may set up a pattern of triangling that continues even when the in-law issue is less important. In-law triangles often pit two women—husband's mother and husband's wife—in conflict over the husband. They start because he is having trouble breaking away, either out of guilt, obligation to his mother, or because he is having difficulty moving toward his wife. He feels the pull intensely; if he pleases one, he automatically displeases the other. Each woman monitors his every move toward the other, keeping a scorecard on his affections. He feels helplessly in the middle of the conflict, and often expects his wife to be more flexible in deference to the older woman.

A wife may also cling to her family-of-origin and be closer to her mother or sister than to her spouse. The reason this is not an issue as often as a triangle involving the husband's wife and his mother is that the husband may quietly distance to his work or friends.

Every group of three does not automatically indicate a dysfunctional communication pattern or triangle. It would be possible for a husband, his wife, and her sister to be in a very good communications pattern. However, in Figure 3-8, the two sisters had always been very close. After the marriage, the wife was not able to get her emotional and companionship needs met by her husband, so she maintains a very close connection with her sister in order to fill up some of her loneliness. Her husband was a distant type of guy who did not like to talk a lot and almost never talked about feelings; he was not upset with the two sisters' being very close. It took the pressure off him; she was getting from her sister what she should have been getting in terms of emotional and companionship time from him.

The triangle shown in Figure 3-8 (next page) describes how the real issue, closeness between the couple, was avoided for a temporary solution. The wife chose not to make her relationship needs clearly known to her husband, probably guaranteeing that they would never be met. The husband, as a result of his wife's movement toward her sister, never had to confront his own difficulties in being more open and communicative. This triangle appears to be stable now, but it will remain that way only as long as the stress and anxiety level of the system remains low.

61

Figure 3-8

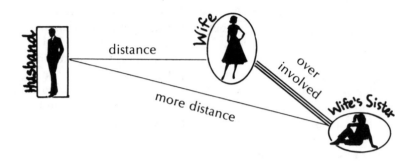

No matter who is involved, the in-law triangle works against the marital dyad, and usually the energy needed to fix it is misplaced in anger at the in-laws. Blaming someone else for a problem takes away the responsibility to make a change, and people generally seek easy solutions whenever possible. Unfortunately, an easy solution in a relationship is often no solution at all.

If you are in an in-law triangle, it is also a good idea to check out your relationships with each of your own parents. Being too close to one of your own parents (or not close enough) can cause you to react more strongly (or not strongly enough) to your spouse's relationships with his or her family of origin. As a rule, triangles with parents and spouses reflect difficulty breaking away from the family of origin, or feeling overresponsible to a parent. Triangles with siblings are more likely to mean an inability to establish closeness with the spouse, or falling into a pattern of maintaining the old closeness with a sibling, rather than going through the effort of establishing closeness in the marriage.

Joe's divided loyalties between his mother and his wife Pat brought her into therapy during the first year of the couple's marriage. The couple had met in college and enjoyed an exciting courtship filled with movies, parties, long walks, and talks. When they married, Joe found a job near his home, and the couple moved within two miles of his parents.

Pat thought her own parents were cold and distant, and had greatly looked forward to joining the close family her husband often spoke about. She was totally unprepared for their reluctance to accept her. While her mother-in-law would be pleasant when

Figure 3-9

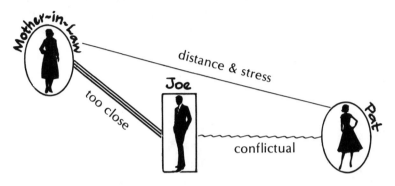

they talked, she spoke repeatedly of her disappointment in her son for marrying so young.

In addition, the couple was expected to join the group twice a week. With both of them working, Pat resented having so much of their leisure time spent with his family. They had frequent fights about the problem, and Pat said sadly that the closeness of their courtship was gone. Recently, a young male co-worker and Pat had become good friends, and she felt herself extremely attracted to him. This feeling frightened her, and she sought therapy.

When Joe joined her for a session, he was relieved to talk openly with the therapist about the pressures he felt from his parents. Apparently, he was almost as shocked as Pat about their behavior because while he had been in school they had been more distant.

This couple was fortunate in being able to address such an issue openly. Many young couples bury such issues, and complicate the situation by adding other triangles, as Pat would have done if she had had an affair with her co-worker.

When a triangle exists, both parties make the third party a scapegoat for the problems in the marital dyad. In the case above, Joe was inclined to agree with Pat that his parents (particularly his mother) were overbearing, and the couple may find closeness in their mutual displeasure with the third party. In-laws are excellent scapegoats, but the catch is that in-law triangles often precede other triangles by setting a pattern for dealing with strife.

2. Child Triangle. If there is an in-law triangle, you can almost predict the development of another triangle. The first child to be born to the above couple will usually be triangled in to balance out the wife's loneliness that she experiences because of her husband's devotion to his mother.

Figure 3-10

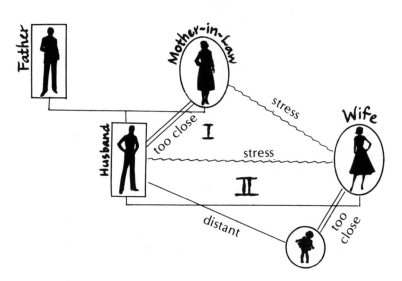

Figure 3-10 illustrates how triangles proliferate in an attempt to achieve some balance in the system. Both triangles **I** and **II** help in some way to calm down the present imbalance in the marital dyad and to get the focus off the closeness issue. The relationships are somewhat calmer because the wife for the time being is less focused on feeling distant from her husband because she is naturally absorbed in mothering. The marital dyad has reestablished some balance, but at a potentially more precarious level of functioning because the issue of closeness for the couple has been put on a back burner. Also demonstrated in Figure 3-10 is the interlocking nature of triangles over generations and how couples can use extended family members (mother-in-law) and their own children to make up for what is missing between them in their marital relationship.

Children make convenient scapegoats, and often a child's misbehavior aims to get Mommy and Daddy to agree on something. The price for all, especially the child, is very high in the most extreme examples of these sorts of triangles.

Children sometimes unwittingly "sacrifice" their lives to keep their parents' marriage together; this is not a conscious or planned process by the youngster. The behavior of the youngster, often an adolescent, serves the purpose of taking the focus off the marital issues and giving the disgruntled husband and wife a common cause to rally around, namely, saving their adolescent.

The intensity of triangles with children often reaches a peak in adolescence as the child begins to break away. If he or she is an important part of the balance of the marital dyad, it can be impossible to leave the family system without great upheaval.

John's family sought therapy at the request of his probation officer. He had dropped out of high school, become a heavy drinker, and compiled a police record for stealing cars.

John, an only child, said he felt close to both his parents, but described their relationship as a "bad marriage." There was, however, a pattern coinciding with Johnny's behavior and that was his parents' history of marital difficulties. When this family came for family therapy, it became obvious to the therapist, and then to the family, that as the couple had more and more trouble in their relationship, the behavior of their son got worse. When asked how the couple resolved the marital issues that they were having, they said that they "had put them aside periodically to try to turn their son around."

The father had actually been thinking of separating around the same time that Johnny's behavior had deteriorated to the point where the police had arrested him. The father said that he felt he couldn't leave at a time like that because he felt that the family needed him and that his wife would not be able to handle Johnny alone.

The triangle depicted in Figure 3-11 illustrates how the husband, wife, and son unwittingly collaborated in maintaining a very dysfunctional situation; the parents did not have to face the real problematic issues in their marriage because Johnny provided them with a serious distraction, and Johnny did not have to face up to his task of becoming a responsible young adult. Johnny also had the feeling—as do most youngsters in this type triangle—

that his rebellious behavior was serving some purpose, although he was not aware of what that was until it was pointed out in the family therapy sessions. This sense of doing something for the family gives the adolescent a feeling of importance and a special place in the family make-up. This is why the adolescent finds it very hard to change that behavior when made aware of it; it is too special a place to give up easily.

Figure 3-11

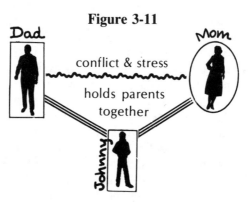

It is important to point out here that the parents are not to blame for John's behavior. They did not make John cut classes or get failing grades; they did not force him to drop out of school; they did not coerce him into drinking, nor did they make him steal the cars. He chose this solution himself. Other troubled children choose the opposite extreme: they attempt to excel at everything. While a child who does this may still have a serious problem later in life, he or she is better equipped to earn a living and find satisfaction in his or her own achievements. They were all caught up in this unwitting process in which everyone pays a price.

3. Sibling–Sibling–Parent Triangle. Siblings will often triangle in a parent or another sibling to cool off a relationship that becomes too hot, too angry, or too close, or a relationship in which one sibling becomes hurt or disappointed. Whatever the problem, it is between the siblings, and parents are in a no-win position. No matter whose side you take in the argument, the other one will be upset with you. The one who calls you in to settle the problem believes that you will side with him or her—otherwise he or she would not have bothered to involve you.

The only reason to intervene is if there is a serious possibility of physical harm, a danger usually overestimated by parents. A parent who continually rescues a child is also preventing that child (often younger or weaker) from learning not to provoke bigger and stronger youngsters. A little "victim" is often a gross provocateur.

Figure 3-12

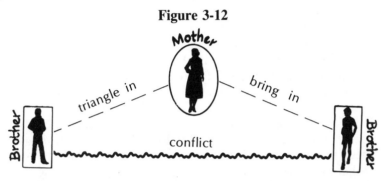

4. Affair Triangle. An extramarital affair is a very explosive triangle indicative that something has gone wrong with the marital relationship. In the affair, one of the parties, instead of looking at the part he or she is playing in the dysfunction of the marital relationship, goes outside the relationship to have his or her needs met. This triangle avoids examining the real issue—the marriage.

Figure 3-13

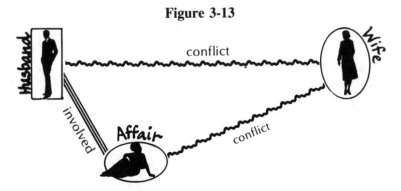

This type of triangle is particularly explosive because when the non-adulterous partner learns of the affair, he or she will generally take a very righteous position—that it is the unfaithful partner's fault entirely. The righteous spouse often misses the point that the marital problem existed before the affair; the affair is only the symptom of the dysfunction of the marital relationship. Instead of talking about what part each played in the dysfunction of the marriage, the righteous spouse blames and often pushes the other spouse away. This is a very difficult triangle to resolve because the righteous spouse now wants to triangle in the affair and talk about the unfaithful partner's deceit, and therefore avoid talking about the state of the marriage before the affair and the part each played in its dysfunction.

5. Alcohol Triangle. Alcohol (a "drinking problem") can sometimes be the third part of a triangle. This type of triangle is one of the more difficult triangles to resolve because the third leg of the triangle is an object (alcohol)—and objects don't change. People can change; when you have three people triangled together, there are more possibilities of where change can take place. People in this triangle constantly talk and argue about alcohol (an object)—projecting the problem onto something else (alcohol)—rather than talking about what is happening between themselves that pushes one of them toward the bottle and away from a person.

By a "drinking problem" I simply mean that alcohol consumption results in difficulties between the spouses. (This type of triangle can result with any substance abuse.) Quantity is not the issue. In this type of triangle, the couple constantly talks about

Figure 3-14

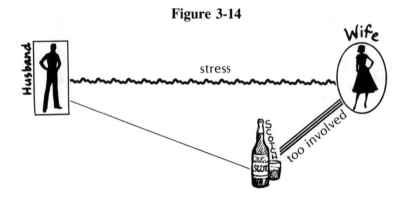

the drinking—as if it were the problem—rather than talking about why drinking is necessary to stabilize their relationship. Drinking in this triangle is generally a symptom of the marital problem, and if one spends every minute talking about the drinking, one will never get to the real issue, which is the marriage. However, it is important to note that once the serious drinking problem has taken hold, dealing with the marriage (or other real issue) is no longer enough to stop the drinking. This is why Alcoholics Anonymous or a detoxification program is often required before the real issue can be dealt with in therapy.

6. Community Activities and Hobbies. Another non-person triangle is the one which forms around the couple and the community involvement of one partner. It could be the PTA, local politics, the women's movement, a charity, the church, or any outside organization which claims a significant amount of attention of one of the spouses. Like commitment to a career, community involvement can give an individual feelings of personal accomplishment that are vital to self-esteem. But organizations that rely on volunteers have an insatiable need for people to carry on their mission, and an essential aspect of any volunteer group is seeking more volunteers. The conscientious citizens who see the genuine need for commitment to issues that affect the entire community or society, in general, feel much internal and external pressure to put in more and more time. The payoffs for such involvement include admiration of others, satisfaction of a need to serve humanity, a way to channel talents not used in one's regular job, and the opportunity to meet new people. All these things contribute to our identity in a positive way.

Hobbies or pastimes are similar in their function and rewards. Running, tennis, golf, swimming, bridge, chess, bowling, watching the stars, gourmet cooking, reading, etc., provide relaxation. Becoming particularly adept at something—running a marathon, winning a bridge tournament—presents opportunities to gain the kind of recognition many people do not get at work. They also provide occasions to meet others with similar interests. On top of all that, they are fun. The need to play is as human as the need for food.

The problem with both community interests and hobbies boils down to time and energy. Obviously, if one partner constantly complains about the other's outside activities, they are in a triangle. At this point, it means sitting down and evaluating priorities. Both parties need to wonder just why this has become an issue. Questions like: Is the involvement a reaction to dissatisfaction with the marriage, or is it a positive search for fulfillment? Is the anger coming out of jealousy, because you or your partner did not take the responsibility to find personal interests? Are there too many other commitments—career demands, young children—also draining necessary energy from the relationship?

Frequently for parents of very young children, community activities quickly become too much of a good thing. This is particularly true if both parents work. Young children demand a great deal of energy from parents because of their physical dependency. Combining child-rearing with work may sap virtually all the resources available, and leave little enough for the marriage, never mind personal interests. Working adults at this stage of family life face difficult decisions about priorities. They need as much—if not more—time off from the demands of children. Yet they experience a triple crunch on their time—marriage, kids, and work. Any extracurricular activity can easily tip the family balance.

No matter what stage of family life a couple is in, they must weigh the very real desire to diversify their lives with interests with the limits on their time. In addition, couples must wonder whether their interests are not a haven from disappointment with the marriage itself.

Mary, a 33-year-old mother of two preschoolers, was referred to counseling by her internist. She felt totally exhausted and had asked the physician for "vitamins." The doctor saw signs of depression and suggested to Mary that she might need more time to herself. Mary replied that she had "every night to herself."

In the first session, Mary spoke reluctantly of her resentment of her husband Bill and his political commitments. She said, "He's not a husband anymore, he's a Democrat." Part of her difficulty in complaining about the situation—he was out three or four nights a week—was that on weekends she enjoyed a lively social life with the people they met through Bill's political affiliations. She spoke enthusiastically about attending the inaugural dinner for the newly-elected governor. She said she also hesitated to complain because they had met as campaign workers, and this interest was something she knew about beforehand. In fact, the interest and his success in this area were still a major attraction.

70

Bill joined Mary for several sessions, in which Mary voiced her fears that she was no longer interesting to Bill, and Bill discussed his feelings that Mary "shut him out" at nights.

This couple soon came up with a compromise. Bill nominated Mary to take his place on one of the committees. Mary found renewed vitality in an old interest, and Bill enjoyed the chance to spend time alone with the children. Not all couples would be able to find such a reasonable solution to this kind of problem. Their interests might not be so mutually compatible in the first place, or there could be a bigger problem in the marriage. Both partners in this case turned out to be fairly flexible, and basically satisfied with marriage and the choice to have children. Couples with more serious doubts about these larger issues may not come to terms so easily. Or, if they do, they may develop a new issue to place between themselves.

Conclusion

These are only a few of the many different types of triangles that can form in close and intense relationships. It is impossible to remain free from all triangles in our relationships. However, triangles in some relationships are more problematic and harmful than in others. To be in a triangle with your spouse is much more serious than with an acquaintance.

Remember, triangles refer to an emotional process that people use in order to avoid the real issue by cooling off an intense situation without making any real change. Try to maintain one-to-one relationships with all the key people in your life; try to make separate time to be with a spouse, children, each of your parents, your siblings, and their spouses. It may take more time but it helps make for more meaningful communications.

References
Bowen, Murray, *Family Therapy in Clinical Practice* (New York: Jason Aronson, 1978).
Fogarty, Thomas F., "Triangles," in *The Family*, Volume 2, No. 2 (1975).

CHAPTER FOUR

The Multi-Generational Family

WE HAVE explored basically how relationships function and malfunction in the family system. There is another important component of the family's system which has been implied all along, but has not been a major focus—what family therapists call the Multi-Generational Transmission Process.* The Multi-Generational Transmission Process refers to the passage of patterns, traditions, values, styles of interaction, and unresolved emotional issues from preceding generations to the present. We have been addressing dyadic and triangular relationships with a focus and emphasis on the nuclear family or the family of procreation; however, each of us also comes from a "family of origin," often referred to as one's "extended family." As such, we actually hold dual, even triple membership; we are members of our own family of origin, our spouse's family of origin, and our own family of procreation. Even if grandparents, parents, or siblings are dead, we all carry around with us a three-generational image of our family.

Probably the single most important factor affecting the functioning level in the family is the quality of the marital relationship of the couple—and the quality of the marital relationships that existed in the extended families of both spouses. Figures 4-1/4-2 suggest that individuals bring into their marriages baggage—patterns, issues, and styles of interaction—from their families of origin.

Everyone comes to marriage with several generations of traditions, myths, patterns, and issues that need to be resolved in order to establish a new husband-wife system. Often these patterns do not emerge until after marriage, because most couples, experiencing the young, immature love of courtship, blind themselves to potential problems that a lifetime commitment will eventually force to the surface. Since it takes two people to collaborate, each partner often obliges the other by overlooking these issues, hoping that the other person will change instantaneously upon saying "I do."

*Murray Brown, *Family Therapy in Cinical Practice* (New York: Jason Aronson, 1978).

72

Figure 4-1

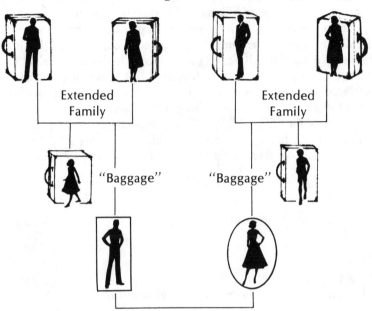

Extended Family

Extended Family

"Baggage"

"Baggage"

Figure 4-2

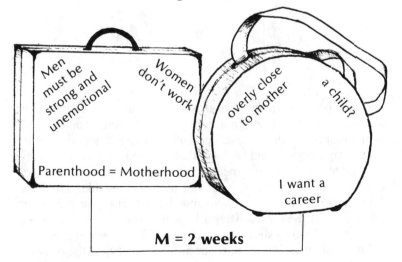

Men must be strong and unemotional

Women don't work

overly close to mother

a child?

Parenthood = Motherhood

I want a career

M = 2 weeks

Once married, the wishful thinking such as "he will stop drinking once we are married" and "I'm sure we will not go to her mother's every Sunday after we are married" no longer works. Reality is at hand, the romantic period is quickly ending, and the wonderful but difficult period of continuing to develop a relationship that can grow has begun. Any troubling issues that may have surfaced during the courtship period and which were promptly swept under the rug come rushing to the surface.

There is the direct "fallout" of a marital relationship to the children in the family (*Figure 4-3*); when the parents are throwing grenades at each other the shrapnel lands on future generations.

Figure 4-3

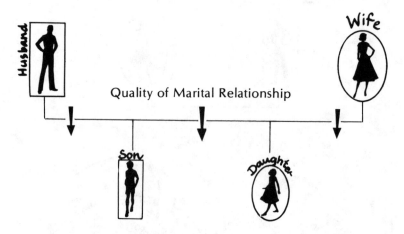

One's point of view about all sorts of issues and behaviors is a product of years spent in a family system. Some opinions fall in the realm of values. A value is an idea or attitude about life, or the way things should be done, that we rate very highly. Having a value about something means that the opinion carries a heavy emotional wallop. Our values lead us to behave like a visiting four-year-old who refuses his sandwich because you didn't cut the crusts off the bread. After all, he reasons, "My mother does it that way," and so should everyone else. This is not to disparage values, only to point out how strongly we hold onto them. After countless repetitions of certain actions, certain ways of responding to stress, we literally have become so accustomed to certain ways that we do not know anything better. Often the first time we encounter anything different is when we marry. During courtship couples may discuss hopes and dreams but often cannot discuss values because they are so deeply entrenched that they are not aware of them until they start living together. The disappointment of trying to live closely with someone with very different values can lead a young couple to develop triangles to handle the stress.

Figure 4-4

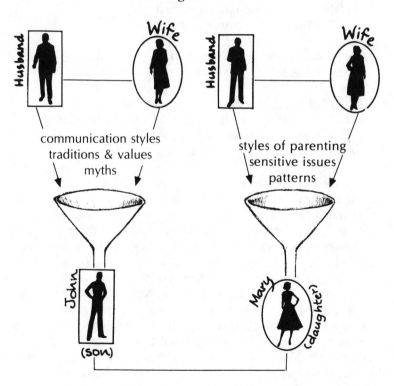

communication styles
traditions & values
myths

styles of parenting
sensitive issues
patterns

In other words, whenever someone is seeking to better understand an interpersonal relationship, it is a good idea to check out one's own attic (family patterns) first.

Often it's easier to observe patterns in your partner's family, just as it's easier to find his or her part in family problems. The temptation would be to point out the difficulties to your partner; however, he or she will probably not appreciate all your trouble. Again, it is better to focus on your own issues with your own parents and siblings. What you observe about your spouse's family will be helpful in understanding how he or she behaves, but understanding a problem does not mean fixing it.

A few examples of the types of patterns and styles that can be passed on are:

—ways of expressing affection or emotion in the family;
—styles of parenting (strict/permissive);
—style of fighting (yelling/not talking);
—holiday traditions.

Some specific patterns that can be transmitted are:

—men shouldn't cry;
—women shouldn't work;
—alcoholism/workaholism;
—fathers being distant from children and mothers being overinvolved with them;
—women being the emotional centers in the family;
—marry your own "kind";

Family patterns repeat themselves; they get passed down through many generations just as family heirlooms do (such as a grandmother's silver tea set). The difference with a family pattern is that it usually is not as obvious as the silver tea set; it is, however, no less real. A pattern develops from one's style or method of acting or interacting with others in the family.

People are usually exposed to a certain emotional role or way of operating in their family of origin. Most of the time we are not aware that it is happening. A son growing up with a father whose relationship style is to seek a lot of time alone, who usually prefers not to talk about his personal feelings, and who would rather work things out by himself is learning a pattern of interaction. If you were to look back a generation at his father's father (the son's grandfather), it would not be surprising to see the same patterns of emotional interaction existing in him, too. These patterns or styles are subtly learned and passed on from one generation to the next, and the only way to change such a pattern is to first understand that it exists.

John and Helen were married for two years. Whenever they had a fight, John would stop talking to her and this "silent treatment" might last a day or even a week. They sought counseling. From interviews with this couple it was learned that John grew up in a home where his father had often used the "silent treatment" when he was angry at his wife or other family members. Helen came from a family where the pattern was, "It isn't good to fight and it's worse to go to bed mad at each other." Thus, when John would stop talking for a few days, Helen's anxiety level would soar; she would become overreactive because she was so uncomfortable with this family pattern, and she would allow the situation to get all out of proportion. To go to bed mad and not talking to each other was equivalent for Helen to starting divorce proceedings.

John reported how he hated it when his father would sit in his big chair and refuse to talk to his mother; he could remember often swearing that he would never be like his father. At first John saw his problem with Helen as different from his parents' situation. He felt Helen was often very unreasonable, saying, "She just wouldn't listen to me." Slowly John began to realize that it wasn't only Helen that he gave this "silent treatment" to. He used to do it to other women that he dated before he was married, to his Aunt Mary (who was the family busybody), and even to some of the people at work. The pattern was beginning to surface but it was difficult for John to accept. To help John see the pattern more clearly, the counselor encouraged him to look at his extended family on his father's side. It wasn't hard for John to remember several instances where his family had gone to visit his paternal grandparents and his grandfather wouldn't talk to anybody. John began to see how this "silent treatment" style had become part of his system. Helen learned that fighting or struggling was not the end of the relationship, but a predictable ingredient in it. By becoming aware of patterns of interactions, both John and Helen were able to make some positive changes in themselves and, consequently, in their relationship.

When an extremely negative pattern has become part of a marital dyad—such as alcoholism—both parties have had prior training that leads them to accept it as the norm. The situation progresses because each member of the dyad experiences something about it as "normal."

Mike, a successful director of regional sales for a pharmaceutical firm, had been arrested for drunken driving, and was going to lose his license. This threatened the family's income, and the judge recommended therapy as an alternative. At this time Sue, his wife of fifteen years, was contemplating leaving him as well.

Mike's pattern of drinking to handle stress had been with the couple since the early years of marriage, but had grown worse after Mike's promotion over a year before. Sue described him as "highstrung," and said that she had never discouraged his drinking before because it made him easier to live with. In the past, when she had suggested drinking might be a problem, they had huge arguments.

Mike's father had been killed in an auto accident—"driving while intoxicated"—when Mike was fourteen. His paternal grandfather was also a problem drinker, and had been in and out of several rehabilitation programs which had limited and sporadic positive effects on him. Obviously Mike's drinking problem wasn't something that just happened to fall out of the sky; it was a familiar pattern used by the men in his family in attempting to deal with stress or in trying to calm some imbalance in their relationship system.

Sue's family history contained no evidence of any drinking problems. The women in her household, however, had a pattern of trying to control the men. Sue was well aware of that pattern but thought that she was different from her domineering mother and aunts. She felt sorry for her father and uncles and thought that she had made up her mind that she was not going to be a controlling and dominant wife. But when Mike drank she did not have to deal with a fully functioning partner, and she had more control in the relationship. Sue was not as obviously domineering as her mother, who would have thrown a drinking husband and his bottles out the door a long time ago; however, in her own laidback style of saying nothing, she manipulated the situation so that she could feel more in control of her husband.

What happens in the marital dyad is that certain patterns of behavior learned in the partners' families of origin fit together to guarantee that the pattern repeats itself. As we noted, people with a pursuing style or an overresponsible style tend to attract their opposites.

There is a similar concept that describes how family systems

Figure 4-5

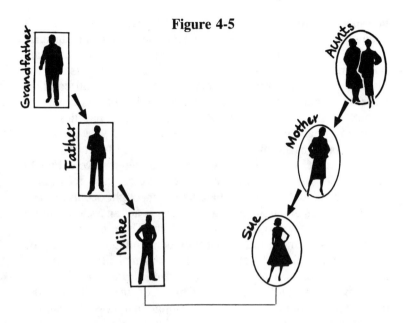

work as a whole. In family systems terms we think of families as having an enmeshed or cut-off style of operating. Enmeshed families believe families should be close, and value spending lots of time together as a group. When there is a conflict, it is generally quite open. If two members are in conflict, the others pressure them to make up. Loud arguments might be common, although they would rarely be about the real issue; they would focus on a particular triangle in the system. These families are apt to express affection openly as well, and be quite physical with one another.

In a distant or cutoff family, members bury conflict, and expression of feelings is taboo. When major conflicts arise, frequently they result in cutoffs. We all know people who after a fight with a family member ceased all communication with that person. Anger is so uncomfortable for these families, they are helpless to share negative feelings in a direct way. If there is a major conflict in a dyad, others may try to act as if it is simply not happening. Within either an enmeshed family or a distant family, there are still distancers and pursuers, but here is where one man's pursuer is another's distancer. For example, a man from an enmeshed family system might see distancing as reading the

79

newspaper in the same room where others were talking. Yet, if a major problem arose, he would join the conflict and only distance after the conflict simmered down. Whereas, a man from a distant family might act out distance by working late four nights a week, playing golf on Saturday and Sunday, and ignoring all conflicts large and small within the rest of the family. Just as opposites attract, it is not unusual for people from cutoff families to be attracted to people from enmeshed families, and vice versa.

Some patterns are more obvious than others. Most of us, if we think about it, can describe whether our parents were openly affectionate with us or with each other. We can also recall how they handled conflict—some parents never fought openly, others made no bones about anger. Family secrets are an area of family life that parents try to hide from children. These topics threaten the family system so much that members collaborate and agree not to mention the subject. Incidents of mental illness, suicide, affairs, and alcoholism are not discussed. Usually, these topics are so intense and toxic that silence does not succeed in lowering the anxiety but builds the tension as though in a pressure chamber until it spills over and affects the entire system. At a certain point, such information can be like the missing link to explain all sorts of behavior and family patterns.

One family hid the fact that a child who died in infancy had Down's Syndrome. The parents never mentioned the child by name, although the mother sometimes spoke of raising five children, rather than four. Everyone in the family cooperated by avoiding the topic and not pressing for any details of the child's illness. The secret came out when a cousin told the spouse of one of the children when she was five months pregnant with her second child.

When finally questioned, the father explained that his reason for not sharing this detail was so that none of the children would be afraid to have children. He also admitted that his wife's grief was so great that even they never talked openly about the child. The pregnant mother's physician reassured her that since the parents had had another healthy child after the Down's baby, her child had no increased likelihood of having the problem.

But this unresolved pain over the child's loss also went a long way to explain the grandmother's annoying habit of "always having to hold the baby," which the younger mother experienced with her first child. Somehow, understanding the woman's grief made this quirk of behavior more tolerable.

Searching for secrets is touchy business, but can generate discussion that ultimately brings family members closer together. The place to start such a search is relatives whose names never come up in the natural course of conversation. Sometimes, as in the case above, a relative less closely connected finds it easier to bring up such an issue. Other times, an aging family member may pass on a vital piece of family history to ensure that it is remembered.

In the life cycle chapter, we will discuss specific tasks of development that accompany various stages of family life. What is useful to keep in mind here is that certain stages of family life may be more or less traumatic because of how that stage went in your family of origin. For example, if you or a sibling was a wild teenager (at least in your parents' eyes), chances are you will approach the adolescent years in your nuclear family with more anxiety than the person whose parents thought their teenage children were "good kids." What might be viewed as a minor problem—a child breaking curfew one night—to one family would spell the beginning of big trouble to another family.

Understanding Family Patterns

One of the best and most graphic ways to explore family patterns and their transmission process from generation to generation is through the use of a genogram. The genogram is a way of taking the family tree and converting it to a relationship road map; it is an organized and systematic diagram of family membership over time. It gives names, ages, dates of events such as births, deaths, marriages, divorces and remarriages and indicates geographical locations, degrees of emotional closeness, and problem areas within the family system. The genogram also shows the developmental states in the family life cycle that different members of the family system are experiencing. As a road map, the genogram looks fixed; however, the lines connecting people symbolize a fluid process of emotional interaction.

The genogram serves many purposes for both the family therapist and the family. Five of its major uses are:

81

1. *Overview*	The genogram gives an overview of family structure and make-up over time. It traces back family chronology and patterns for three or four generations.
2. *Relationships*	The genogram charts biological connections and relationships through marriage. It clearly helps one see who is related to whom and how.
3. *Roots*	Looking at one's genogram can give one a real sense of one's origin and beginnings. It helps one to trace and understand the process of being connected over time.
4. *Graphic*	The genogram provides a visual tool for tracing patterns.
5. *Family Life Cycle*	By looking at the genogram, one is able to get a sense of the different life cycle stages that many of the family members could be experiencing.

Constructing a Genogram

Figure 4-6 illustrates all the symbols needed to make a genogram. Let's construct a genogram of the Jones family and use this tool as a way of showing the intergenerational connectedness in families and how families pass patterns on from one generation to the next.

Rob, Jr., and Mary Jones have been married for twenty-two years, have two children: Rob, III, who is 19 and living in Europe, and Julie, who is 14. They have been living in Connecticut since they married. Rob met Mary in New York while they were both in college.

Figure 4-6

Genogram Chart*

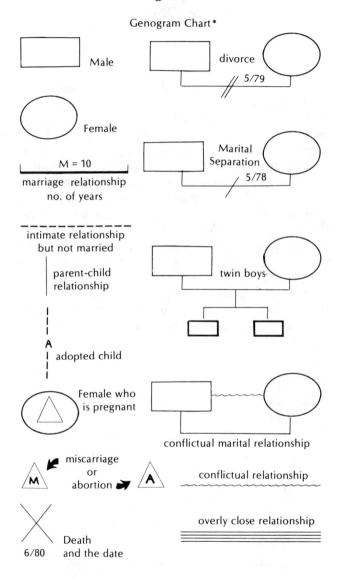

* Murray Bowen, M.D.

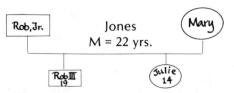

The above drawing is the genogram of just the nuclear family; since both Rob, Jr., and Mary have a family of origin of their own, let's add those parts to create the total system.

Rob is 45, the oldest of two children, born in Los Angeles, California, to Rob, Sr. (70), and Marge Jones (68). Rob's sister Cathy is 40, lives in Dallas, Texas, with her husband Bill (42) and their daughter Margaret (10). Rob, Jr., has had a very conflicted relationship with his father for many years. Robert, Sr., was a successful, self-made executive whose drive, determination and long hours of hard work catapulted him to the presidency of his firm. His travel and business commitments gave him little time to be with his family. Rob, Jr., resented this absence and, as a result, made himself scarce when his father was home or when his father tried to be a father. This was part of Rob's reason for leaving California to attend college in New York.

The figure following has added Rob, Jr.'s, family of origin to the genogram.

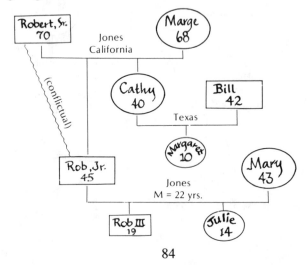

84

The following genogram graphically depicts Mary's extended family which is described in the following paragraph.

> Mary (43), on the other hand, is an only child, raised in Boston, Massachusetts, by Joe (68) and Regina (64) Reilly. The Reillys were a close Irish, Catholic immigrant family. Mary was very close to her mother and often worried about her health. Joe was much more of a loner who enjoyed being out with the boys. In contrast to Rob, Mary found it difficult living as far away as she did from her parents. She often wanted Rob and the kids to visit her parents in Boston.

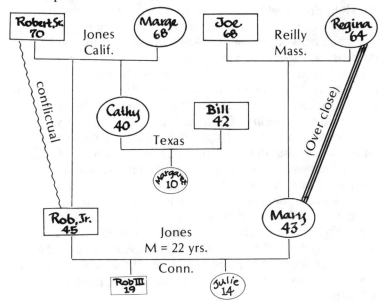

Genograms Tell Us a Lot

In order to fully understand a family one must develop a perspective that includes several generations. The reason for this is that patterns of behavior and ways of feeling are passed—knowingly and unknowingly—from one generation to the next. Patterns include ways of relating, interacting, showing affection, and getting angry. They include attitudes toward money, sex, work, leisure time, religion, parenting, and numerous other issues and traditions.

We will now look at the Jones family genogram and, from the information available, examine two family patterns that are repeating themselves.

1. Father–Son Conflict. Robert, Sr., and Rob, Jr., had a conflictual relationship. The information at hand indicates that the father at one point had little time left over from his career endeavors to spend with his son; the son reciprocated by distancing from the father when the father tried to make time for his son. Finally, he moved across country to get away from his father's influence. Rob, Jr., who received little fathering from his own father, found it difficult to give the closeness to his son, Rob, III. Rob, Sr., taught distance to Rob, Jr., by not knowing how to better balance his career pursuits and his relationship with his son while he was growing up; Rob, Jr., showed that he learned the distance lesson by giving it back to his father when his father belatedly tried to move closer, and again when he moved 3,000 miles away to go to school. And now, Rob, III, has been in Europe for two years, rarely writing to anyone in his family.

2. Mother–Daughter Relationship. "Only" children generally feel and have exerted upon them a greater pull within the family system; they often experience a heightened sense of responsibility for their parents' happiness, and often live nearer to them. The pull in the system might be expressed in terms of overinvolvement by one or both of the parents in the life of the only child, or it might be felt by the child as having to meet all the expectations and wishes of the parents. When there is a problem in a family with an only child, the issue generally revolves around overcloseness and an inability to properly separate. In these situations the thought of moving away or leaving home˙ stirs great emotional upheaval.

In the case of Mary Jones, there is obviously a strong pull between her and her mother. Regina began to devote a lot of her emotional energy—which might normally have been going to Joe—to her daughter. Mary received a lot of attention because her mother, so to speak, had no one else with whom to share her emotional energy. Mary probably enjoyed receiving all this attention as a child, but a pattern was developing which made it hard during adolescence for Mary to separate and not feel overly responsible for her mother.

A similar situation is developing for Julie, who up until now has been a delightful daughter to her mother. With the onset of adolescence, she is having an enormous power struggle with her mother as she tries to move out more on her own. This is not unusual; when a parent has had a difficulty with a particular issue in his or her own life, like independence from mother, it is quite common to find that same issue reappearing in the next generation when that parent's own child is at the same developmental stage.

Increased Stress from the Multi-Generational Triangle

The multi-generational triangle is a concept used to describe how a dysfunctional communications process learned in one generation gets passed on to the next with the additional complication being that the pattern has usually gotten worse over time. Figure 4-7 indicates how one pattern—an overclose mother-daughter relationship represented by the numbers 1, 2, 3, 4—has repeated itself over the generations in an attempt to make up for the closeness that was lacking in the marital dyad, resulting in more dysfunction in each succeeding generation. The heavy dark lines in Figure 4-7 represent the three-generational triangle (3) that is occurring, and the dotted lines represent each separate generational triangle.

In the initial triangle the problem is that the spouses are "not close" to each other, and child #2 is used in balancing out what was missing in the marital dyad. Child #2 grows up experiencing this environment, which lacks closeness and teaches that a close parent-child relationship can substitute for closeness in the marital relationship. By the time she marries, not only has she not learned how to develop closeness in relationships, but also she is more frustrated and impatient with its absence; and this leads to a more conflictual marriage. Child #3 tries to make up for what is lacking in her parents' dyad, but she also is unsuccessful in this role and she learns little from her parents about closeness. When child #3 marries, and closeness is not achieved, the intensity from the years of dysfunction over trying to develop intimacy has grown so strong that the relationship ends in divorce. Child #4, single, 42 years old and still living at home, is depicted as depressed and isolated; it looks as though she isn't even going to bother pursuing closeness.

Figure 4-7

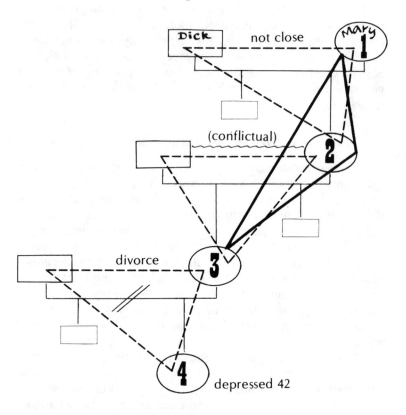

The patterns in these multi-generational triangles are very strong. Awareness of their existence is the first step in getting control over and changing these patterns.

Reactive Patterns—"Opposites Are the Same"

Sometimes patterns can be quite intense—so much so that someone in the succeeding generation reacts to the existing pattern by deciding to do just the opposite. This usually is not much better because it often is not a free choice toward something but rather a reactive stance away from something else.

Figure 4-8 shows what could happen if a daughter reacted to

her mother's dominant style by being permissive and distant. She would explain the development of her style of parenting by saying that her mother was *too* possessive and smothering, so she wants to put space between herself and her daughter so that her daughter will have some room to breathe.

Figure 4-8

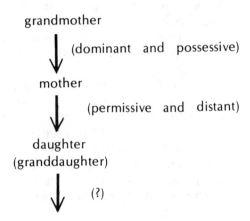

The granddaughter (daughter) might say that her relationship with her mother was unsatisfactory because her mother's permissiveness and distance seemed to lack concern and affection. The dissatisfaction in the mother-daughter relationship from one generation to the next might remain the *same*, that is, unsatisfactory.

The passage of patterns from one generation to the next often swings like a pendulum—from one extreme to the other. One generation becomes so highly reactive or charged to the patterns, styles, or behaviors of the previous generation that the next does a 180-degree turnabout.

Another example of how "opposites are the same" is when teetotaling and alcoholism flip-flop from one generation to the next (*Figure 4-9*). Both styles are at the opposite end of the spectrum, that is, one drinks too much and the other never takes a drink; yet, they are the same in that they are both struggling with the issue of control of alcohol consumption. The alcoholic has no control over his/her drinking, and the teetotaler has

89

assumed a position of rigid overcontrol as a reaction to the fear of inability to control drinking in moderation. You seldom find a teetotaler in a family system where there hasn't been a drinking problem because teetotaling is a reactive stance to the fear of losing control. Teetotaling is far better for the liver than alcoholism, but they are both symptoms and signs that stress is present to a significant degree in the family; they are just two different styles of attempting to cope with the issue of control. Thus establishing a rigid and overcontrolling pattern or style of action to deal with stress is not the best solution; it just looks better than having no control during stressful periods.

Unfortunately, what happens in many cases where people have chosen the extremes is that a person takes his/her style of dealing with alcohol (that is, rigid control or no control at all) and begins to generalize and apply that approach toward coping with stress to other areas, such as childrearing, dealing with fellow employees, and handling interpersonal relationships. With some awareness one can see that doing the complete opposite need not be a better approach and that a more balanced style, something between no control and rigid overcontrol, would be better.

Figure 4-9

Thus as we build our notion of the family operating as a system of multiple people and complex factors, no person or event can be viewed in isolation, but must be seen in a multi-generational context in order to be fully understood. Family patterns have been known to influence styles of relating, choice of mate and selection of a career. It is important to remember that there is nothing wrong with repeating or continuing a pattern; if it works it should be continued. The point to be aware of is that many patterns that do not work often get repeated and passed on. This occurs for many reasons, but one major reason is that patterns that we grow up with we then become familiar with and accustomed to. If you have been exposed to a pattern for twenty years before leaving home, there is a strong chance that you will be affected in some way by it and, therefore, carry it or some reaction to it with you into your future relationships. Awareness of the multi-generational transmission process is a first and vital step. Some of the patterns and roles that we have are fine, and we wouldn't want to change them; others we might like to change immediately.

How the Family Operates as a System

In order to view the family as a system, one must begin to expand the parameters by which he/she defines "family." To a person who thinks in terms of systems, a family is not an isolated group consisting of some combination of a mother, father and/or child; rather, "family" encompasses a much broader and more complex network of people, issues, events, and variables that have been interacting both knowingly and unknowingly with each other over several generations. This is why families and family members cannot be fully understood if viewed in isolation; they must be viewed in the context of their family history over time.

Although this concept of viewing the family as a system seems to be logical, most people during periods of stress within their family tend to develop tunnel vision; they look for one person to blame or single out as being the cause of all the problems in the family. In addition to looking at dyads, and triangles, and the patterns we learned in our family of origin, it is also valuable to check out other branches of the family tree when trying to track down the true cause of a problem.

There are varying degrees of connectedness between grown children and their parents and siblings. This has a lot to do with culture, geography, stage in the life cycle, and quality of the relationship. Some families stay in good contact while others drift apart; some families visit often while others never do. As a family therapist, I encourage family members to strive to become separate from their families of origin but to remain connected to them. This requires, at times, a lot of effort, but I think that it is crucial for healthy family functioning. I often compare a family member's emotional connectedness to his or her family of origin to the functioning of a human heart. The human heart functions best when all the connectors (the veins and arteries) are in good working order and free from blocks and obstructions. An emotional system functions best when we are well connected to all the other members in the family system. Just as the heart will have an "attack" if a connector becomes blocked or cut off, so will the emotional system be vulnerable to attack if family members cut off contact or allow emotional connectors to be blocked.

Sometimes the effect of an event in a sibling's life or a parent's life involves increased responsibilities. Many of you may, for instance, be guardians for the children of one of your siblings. In the unlikely event of the sibling's premature death, your nuclear family might add one or two (or more) members overnight. Or, again, in the case of parental illness, you may have to add visiting or certain caretaking functions into your current life.

Other times our involvement is peripheral as far as what we have to do about it, but intense in an emotional way. This is because the events in the lives of other family members have meaning for us. An issue that lies dormant in our minds for years can suddenly flare up because of an incident in the extended family. This often happens because we seem to absorb loss and disappointment in stages, and when we can, we put our attention elsewhere. So, for example, an unmarried adult in his or her 20s may not think about this issue much and instead focus attention on career issues. But each time a sibling marries it serves as a reminder. Most people don't decide to never marry; they put it off, or are searching for the right partner. The older the unmarried sibling gets, the more the marriage of a sibling, or even a cousin, may affect him or her. This is not to say, in the case of remaining single, that the person should despair at the prospect of living life alone. Rather, as other members of the family do marry he or she will be reminded more strongly of singleness versus wedded bliss. So a bachelor in his late 30s, who was dating a woman he cared for, might think more seriously about marriage if his favorite cousin was to "tie the knot", than if no one close to him were to marry at that time. A similar effect might be had on childless couples who were putting off the final decision of whether or not to have a child. Seeing a tiny baby belonging to a sibling puts the issue back in the pool of current thoughts to be sorted out, and decisions to be made.

Also, although we may not expect concrete help from parents or siblings, they can still disappoint us terribly by not giving us the emotional support we expect at certain times. It is this disappointment that may lead us to break away from having any closeness or expectations of them and, perhaps, to seek distance from them in triangles.

Consider the effect on the family's equilibrium in the example below when an event occurs. Jim and Mary Brown happily announced the birth of their first child, which for them is very positive news. Jim's parents were delighted, especially his father, as the baby is the first male grandchild and Mr. Brown felt relieved, after four granddaughters, that the "Brown" family name would be preserved. Jim's older brother Bill, the proud father of four girls, was happy for Jim and Mary, but his own unresolved feelings about not having a son were stirred up.

Mary's mother had a different reaction. Mary is the youngest of eight, her mother already has 17 grandchildren, and Mary was crushed by the lack of excitement and enthusiasm that her mother showed, particularly in contrast to Jim's parents' reactions. Mary's oldest and closest sister, Jean, who is single, 34 years old, and a successful executive for a large corporation, became very distant. The birth rekindled Jean's feelings about not being married, not having children, and her career. She wanted some time and space to sort this out, while Mary felt hurt by not having closeness and sharing right away. Also, Mary's memories of her father, who died five years earlier, were rekindled as she saw resemblances of her father in her new son. She was quite sad at the realization that her father would never see her child. This example shows how a very positive event for two people in a family can stir positive and mixed emotions in several members throughout the entire system.

Although Jim and Mary were very close during the pregnancy, the normal stress of caring for the new baby was coupled with

Mary's disappointment in her mother and sister's reaction, and her renewed grief. Jim's older brother's negative reaction did not affect Jim, and he was unsympathetic that Mary was so concerned about what "they" (the mother and sister) thought. He felt cheated out of his joy by Mary's sadness; he subsequently started to seek distance from Mary by working more hours at his new job in a law firm. Only when Mary became depressed enough to seek therapy did the couple see how this pattern had started.

The larger family system is particularly vulnerable to major events—births, marriages, deaths and divorces. These events all relate to adding or losing a family member. Even at a distance they demand our attention. Whereas from across country, you might only be vaguely aware that your brother and his wife were having a rough time with their teenage daughter, if she got engaged in her senior year of high school and decided not to go to college (as everyone expected), you would feel more concerned. The closer we are physically and emotionally to our families of origin, the smaller the event needed to have a direct effect on our lives. With a sister in another town you might be called upon to listen or give advice when she argues with her husband now and again. With a sister five states away or one you don't see socially, you may not hear about it until the arguments reach crisis proportion.

We will see in the life cycle chapter that there are several stages of family life that require shifts, and include these sorts of major events, but also involve the more subtle tasks of allowing children to progress from one stage of development to another. In this chapter, we want to focus on current events in the extended family which may be affecting the balance in your nuclear family. To do this, we want to review five basic concepts of family functioning, and apply them to the workings of the larger family system.

1. *The actions of one person in the system affects everyone else in the system.* The family functions as an emotional system or unit that is uniquely attuned to the feelings and behaviors of all members in the system; this is not to say that everyone will be affected in the same way or to the same degree but, rather, everyone will have some sort of reaction.

2. *Every family has its own unique balance or equilibrium.* As I said earlier in Chapter 2, all families strive to attain a balance in their family and relationship systems because when the family

is "in balance" (at rest), anxiety is usually lower. Thus, a family is said to be in balance when the relationships and roles that have been established within the family are accepted, at least for the present time, by all its members. If, however, one family member decides to make a change, the family balance will be upset. The term "family balance" should not be understood to mean "good working order" or taken as a comment about the functioning level of the family. It refers more to a state of equilibrium that has been reached by the family, in which there is usually a reduction of tension, but not necessarily better functioning.

3. *Chain reactions occur in family systems and tend to repeat themselves.* Since the actions of everyone in a family affect every other person in that system, and since these actions send ripples through the family changing the family balance, the process can best be described as a "chain reaction." Figure 4-10 depicts this family when it is without stress and in balance; each circle represents a metal ball which is hung from a balance beam; and when one of the metal balls moves, it strikes the metal ball next to it, thus sending a charge or ripple through every ball in the system.

Figure 4-10

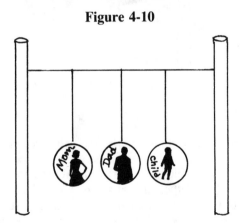

Figure 4-11 (next page) shows the family system after stress has entered. Chain reactions will repeat themselves until one member detaches himself or herself from the emotional arena in which they occur.

4. *There are neither good guys nor bad guys in a family.* It is

important when trying to understand how a family is operating to avoid classifying or labeling members as good or bad, because in some way everyone in the family is part of the problem and part of the solution. It is quite common for families to try to isolate one member as "the problem" or "the bad one" because that seems to get everyone else off the hook. Most people are able to see the part they play or contribute when things are functioning well in a family, but it's more difficult for people to see, understand, and accept the part they play when there is a problem.

Figure 4-11

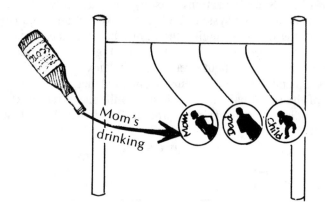

5. *Problems are not in people but between people.* Family problems exist in the relationship network between people; for example, when a couple is having a marital problem, the problem is not "housed" in either one of them, but rather it is between them and gets in the way of their achieving more closeness (*Figure 4-12*, next page). If relationship problems were "in" people, surgery would be the simple solution, but obviously, no one goes to a surgeon for a relationship problem.

The trouble with viewing a relationship problem as being "in" somebody else is that it means that one person has total responsibility for the problem and the other person has none—one is the villain and the other the saint.

Figure 4-12

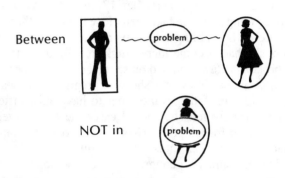

John and Ruth York have been married for 20 years and are living in New Jersey. A graphic representation of what is happening in their family appears in Figure 4-13.

Figure 4-13
York Family Genogram in 1983

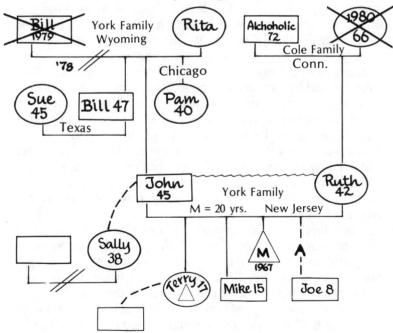

The York family presented the family problem as their pregnant teenage daughter, Terry. Terry, at 17, was the York's oldest child. As a young girl, she had been close to her mother, helping to take care of her siblings. However, during the past three or four years she had become increasingly rebellious. She had frequently broken curfew, and had on several occasions been caught smoking marijuana. Now that she was pregnant, she wanted to keep her child. Her father wanted her to have an abortion, and her mother strongly felt she should carry the fetus to term and give the baby up for adoption. (Note: The Yorks had adopted a child that they had taken in as a foster child.)

In taking the family's genogram, it became apparent that the current problem was part of a chain reaction of events that started with the death of John's father four years earlier. Two factors added to the normal stress of this event for John. First, there was enormous geographic distance between John and the other members of his family of origin. None of them were able to offer or receive the kinds of support that only immediate family members can give each other in such a situation. Second, John had been what we typically think of as a "middle child" in his family of origin. He was a rather wild teenager himself, and had been the focus of many family arguments. His grief was combined with feelings of guilt for not having been a "better son."

John and Ruth had always had a conflictual relationship, which John handled by working long hours. However, for a time, Ruth was more nurturing and sympathetic to John, and he felt closer to her than he had in years. But the following year, Ruth's mother died. Ruth had no siblings, and her family lived in Connecticut, which was only a two-hour drive from their home. Her mother had been overresponsible in the relationship with her alcoholic father, and Ruth now felt pulled to take up where she left off. Ruth's emotional energies turned away from John toward her own grief and her father.

While John tried to understand this at first, his own disappointment led him to start an affair with Sally, a colleague at work. Sally, 38, was recently divorced, and not interested in remarriage, but wanted a close emotional connection. Ruth was suspicious of their friendship, but hesitated to confront the issue directly.

Terry, it turned out, had become sexually active within several months of the father's affair. It would be hard to say how Terry's budding sexuality had influenced her father's choice. People in midlife are apt to be reminded of their own sexuality as their children approach sexual awareness. It would also be hard to say whether Terry chose to seek closeness with a peer in premature sexual activity because her parents were too wrapped up in their own grief, or because at some level she felt the sexual tension in her father.

At any rate, once John and Ruth became more aware of the chain reaction of family members, they ceased being so angry at Terry for her predicament and began to see the multiple stresses in the family system. With the anger defused, each was able to give Terry an opinion and allowed her to make her own decision. Terry chose to have the child, and give it up for adoption. Obviously the fact that her younger brother was adopted meant that Terry carried with her a strong value about adoption, which made it more likely for her to make this choice than another young woman whose family had never adopted a child. Both her parents were able to support her decision.

As Virginia Satir has said in *Peoplemaking*, "family life is something like an iceberg."* There is a real similarity between a "family system" and an iceberg; the smaller and visible tip of the iceberg represents the family members in the system and the larger, hidden, more complex and dangerous part of the iceberg represents the inner and sometimes less obvious workings of the "system" (*Figure 4-14*). The system consists of family traditions

Figure 4-14

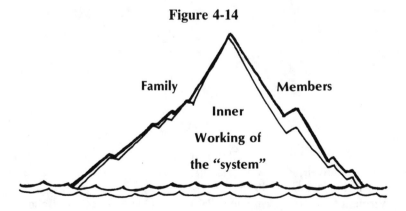

*Virginia Satir, *Peoplemaking* (Palo Alto, CA: Science and Behavior Books, Inc., 1972).

and family patterns, such as overresponsibility, underfunctioning and lack of closeness.

The system contains all the family secrets and taboo topics that people tiptoe around for decades; it contains the unexpressed needs and feelings of the family system's members, and it consists of a family process that has been going on for generations. The better one understands the system, the less likely will be the chance of a shipwreck and the more likely the chances for closeness, improved communication, and better relationships.

References
Murray Bowen, *Family Therapy in Clinical Practice* (New York: Jason Aronson, 1978).
Virginia Satir, *Peoplemaking* (Palo Alto, CA: Science and Behavior Books, Inc., 1972).

CHAPTER FIVE

The Family Life Cycle

AS YOU probe your family's past and present in search of the reasons why it operates the way it does, there is one more angle of family functioning I'd like you to consider. This angle is what Betty Carter and Monica McGoldrick refer to as "the family life cycle."* They designated six developmental stages (*Figure 5-1*) and have defined the tasks that must be accomplished at each of these stages in order for the family and its members to successfully move on to the next stage.

Figure 5-1
(Carter and McGoldrick, 1980)*

Stage 1   Between Families: The Unattached Young Adult

Stage 2   The Joining of Families through Marriage:
             The Newly Married Couple

Stage 3   The Family with Young Children

Stage 4   The Family with Adolescents

Stage 5   Launching Children and Moving On

Stage 6   The Family in Later Life

Each stage involves different tasks for different members of the family; for example, the young adult has the task of becoming autonomous while at the same time the parents have the task of encouraging independence and "letting go."

We are all aware that children go through stages. In fact, how often do we reassure each other with "it's only a stage" as we share the trials and tribulations of parenting? In recent years we have also become more aware that adults continue a developmental process with stages of its own. Authors Daniel Levinson in *The Seasons of a Man's Life* and Gail Sheehy in *Passages*

---

*E. A. Carter and M. McGoldrick, *The Family Life Cycle: A Framework for Family Therapy* (New York: Gardner Press, Inc., 1980).

popularized this theory. However, family systems are made up of adults and children whose lives and stages intersect. Together, they have a developmental process as a family—the family life cycle.

A family's growth is really a combination of the tasks of the adult members and the child members. In the family, each member has tasks to be completed at each stage, and when this is not accomplished these unresolved issues (that old emotional baggage) make the next stage even more difficult for the family and the individual. Each stage demands that every member adapt in some way. Because family members are all connected, any one member's failure to do his part affects the whole group.

These transitions in family development can begin with a change in only one family member's status yet, as we have seen, require that all family members adjust as well. For example, the fifth stage of the family life cycle, Launching Children, begins when the first child leaves home. This one member's exit means every other member of the system begins a new phase of family living that will ultimately leave the parents alone for the first time in years and means the addition of new family members as children marry. Family members must accept themselves and each other as different because they've grown older and are ready to take on new tasks. The difficulty is that a family system prefers to maintain the status quo rather than make a change of any kind— good, bad or indifferent.

These life cycle changes also drastically affect the structure of a household. In one stage, The New Couple, the household has two members. In the next stage, The Couple with Young Children, it has three or more. At this stage, parents must watch their offspring's every move, and then they must learn to allow children greater responsibility for themselves in the next phase, The Family with Adolescents. Eventually, the structure is back to two, after the Launching Children phase is completed and, when one spouse dies, to one. Changes in family structure also bring new faces and personalities. With marriage, there is also a new set of family patterns to be absorbed into the family system.

With all this shifting comes a specific task that characterizes each stage of the family life cycle. The very nature of a task puts it in the realm of work—a job to be accomplished, not overnight but over a period of months and years. This family work means one family member taking a step forward, another a step backward, and a third a step to the side. Since we all tend to be uncomfortable during this period of imbalance, many families experience greater anxiety during these times than during what we might call "rest periods," when the family has achieved a new balance.

In other words, the most perfectly healthy family imaginable would still experience stress as the family enters a new phase of the life cycle. Members are feeling unsure of themselves and unsure of how to treat each other. The various dyads are particularly vulnerable because partners react differently to the changes. For example, in the Launching Children phase, a mother may be relieved to have some free time and a father may feel great sadness at having missed his children's childhood. He may try to move closer to her and resent her new interests outside the home at the same time she's saying "after all these years, it's about time I had some freedom."

Family therapists see the stresses surrounding the tasks of the different stages of family development as normal and predictable; they often divide them into horizontal and vertical stresses (*Figure 5-2*). If you were to imagine a family moving along a straight line, these horizontal stresses would be like hurdles the family must overcome as members are born, grow older, leave home, marry, have their own children, and eventually die. Other horizontal stresses are the events in the larger society that present additional hurdles in the course of a lifetime. A good example would be a major economic recession.

Another major horizontal stress in present family life has been the women's movement. Changing roles and increased numbers of working mothers mean that more husbands and wives are working on a different kind of marital dyad than their parents had. Since they have no model for this kind of marriage, it seems unfamiliar and leaves the couple more vulnerable to stress and conflict. Changing values on sexuality and drug use also affect the family as it moves along its course, particularly during the adolescent and launching stages when the younger generation breaks away from the family of origin.

In addition, the family also has vertical stresses. Vertical implies an up-and-down movement, and vertical stress refers to the

Figure 5-2

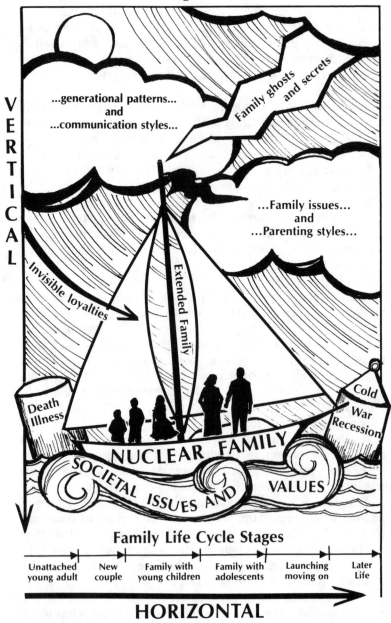

multi-generational transmission process, the past and present effect of three generations of the family's system upon each other's lives. This includes the various triangles, patterns, values, myths, and secrets of the family of origin and the effect of current events in each generation on branches of the family tree.

As we have seen, past patterns learned in the family of origin influence the nuclear family, our family of procreation. As we go from one stage of the family life cycle to another, it is also useful to understand how that stage went in our family of origin. So, for example, if your spouse's family had significant trouble in the New Couple stage, and your parents had difficulties at the Launching Children phase, both of these stages may carry more than the usual amount of stress for you and your spouse when you get there. In fact, it is where we might envision the horizontal stresses and the vertical stresses meeting that families are likely to have their greatest problems.

With enough family stress—from both horizontal (normal life cycle movement) and vertical (generational) factors—any family could get stuck or get knocked off the track. A new railroad need not be built when this happens; the train needs only to be helped to get back on track so that it can begin again to negotiate the life cycle tasks that lie ahead.

When one is able to view the family's course from both horizontal and vertical perspectives, one is able to understand that family upset is a normal part of every family's life and that there is predictable family upset during particular life cycle stages (for example, adolescence). One knows that a family experiencing stress is neither "bad" nor "sick," but rather that it is temporarily "stuck" in making the transition from one phase to the next. Families are unique; some will have trouble making the transition from one stage to the next while others will have none at that particular stage. It is normal to get "stuck" in transition from one life cycle stage to another.

Family therapists often work with families who are "stuck" or who are having trouble making the transition from one stage of the family life cycle to the next. Without a doubt, many of you reading this book are experiencing the natural family upheaval caused by the progress of your family from one stage to the next. The greatest stress is likely to be at the point where each specific stage actually begins, before the family gets accustomed to the new way it has to operate. Although only one member may be showing the signs of the whole family's problem, if the whole group gets on the track, everyone will feel more comfortable.

In each stage there will be one emotional issue and several tasks that need to be accomplished in attempting to move on to the next stage. Let's set up a diagram (*Figure 5-3*) that can serve as a model in which 1.) the circular wheel represents the central emotional issue that needs to be dealt with during the transition from one stage to the next and 2.) the spokes identify the tasks to be accomplished and the changes in family relationships, structure, status, and membership that are necessary in order to move on successfully to the next stage.

Figure 5-3

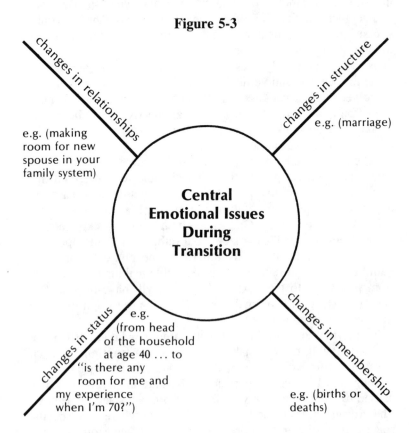

While the actual task that needs to be accomplished can be understood by explaining the goals of the particular stage, the whole process is important to keep in mind. This is because a problem in one stage has usually had its roots in the problems of another stage. A whole family may feel stuck because the last child refuses to move out of the house; something that was scheduled to happen—all the children out on their own—isn't happening. The specific task is to help the adult child leave home, to separate, and to enter the Unattached Young Adult stage. But to understand the cause, it may be necessary to look back at the New Couple stage, or the parents' own Unattached Young Adult phase. Again, the idea is to move outside the strongest complaint of the moment, and the person most likely to be blamed, and get some distance from the problem by understanding its origins. Studying the tasks of the life cycle is another way to see how the family works and where the trouble spots may lie.

It is important to point out that one stage does not end abruptly and then another stage begins without connection to the prior stage. On the contrary, there is an overlapping between the stages whereby one is not only working on the tasks and issues of the stage that one is leaving but one is also preparing for the tasks of the stage that lies just ahead. Likewise, the tasks of the previous stage are never completely finished but must be constantly worked and reworked as situations arise and changes occur in the system over time. For example, no one ever completely finishes the task of separating from family of origin by the time of marriage; this task surfaces over and over again in the next several stages, but the manner in which one has dealt with this in the previous stage will have a significant effect on how one handles it in each succeeding stage. If the young adult had trouble leaving his/her family of origin in stage one, then it would be predictable that in stage two that same young adult might have trouble putting his/her new spouse ahead of the family he/she has just left.

Unattached Young Adult—Stage 1

Each stage of the life cycle has one major focus, with several subtasks. The main issue in the Unattached Young Adult stage is the separation of the young adult from his or her family of origin. This first stage of family life is actually the entire goal of

107

Figure 5-4

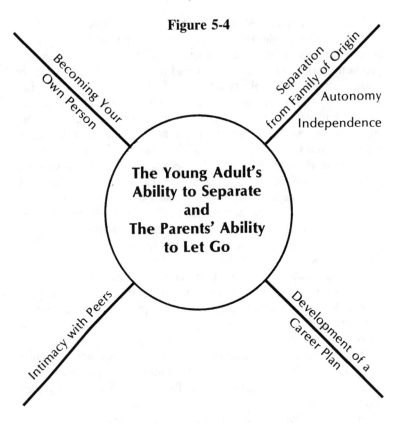

raising children. We want to give our children the security they need to be able to eventually leave us, but still stay emotionally connected to us.

This stage is to me the most important and it often does not receive adequate attention because many young adults feel pressure to get married within some socially acceptable time frame, thus not giving this very important "unattached" stage enough time. How often have we heard, "Is he/she married yet?" as though it is a magical state that everyone has to reach by a certain date. The question is asked as though marriage is seen as a solution to something rather than as a beginning. Although young adults are marrying somewhat later (McGoldrick, p. 95), family pressures, societal norms and, for women, their own biological time clocks, are still adding pressure on the young adult to move out of the "unattached" stage too quickly.

Separation from Family of Origin. There are some very important tasks to be accomplished in this stage and they all take time. The young adult has just come out of adolescence, which for most has been a turbulent time. It was during this period that we all began to separate from our families of origin, which involved questioning our parents' life style, values, knowledge and interests, while at the same time establishing our own identities. This process usually gets stormy and is seldom completed by the time adolescence ends. Separation is a very difficult process and often adolescence is only the beginning attempt to accomplish it. The young adult has a chance to accomplish a much more mature separation if he/she knows that this is the primary task of this stage.

Becoming Your Own Person. The "unattached" period is a time for reassessing, evaluating, and taking stock of what one has taken or received from one's own family of origin (values, issues and styles of interacting) and what one plans to keep or discard and how one plans to use or adapt what one keeps. This is a very important task that many people never accomplish because they are off into the second stage of being a couple before they realize what type of baggage they are bringing with them to the relationship. The myth that love conquers all or that problems can be worked out later does not correlate well with the latest divorce statistics. It is always more difficult, but not impossible, to try to get it together later.

There is a tremendous amount of reactive behavior that takes place while young adults try to separate from their parents. People move from the East Coast to the West in an attempt to get away from the emotional pull or wishes of their parents; unfortunately, geographical distance does not equal emotional maturity. Some people will marry in an attempt to leave home in a way that is acceptable to their parents, while others will marry someone completely unacceptable to the family as a way of attempting to separate. These types of marriages usually have stormy times ahead because the primary task of the first stage, which was to emotionally separate, was never accomplished.

Development of a Career Plan. Theodore Lidz in *The Person* (1968) emphasizes that the two most important decisions to be made by the young adult involve occupational and marital choice.

He also believes that the degree of separation from one's parents greatly affects our choice of both. The task for all young people is to make a choice of career based on their interests and talents. A son should not become a doctor because his mother has planned on it since the day he was born, and a daughter should not be an actress because her fundamentalist Christian parents would die if she did. This does not mean that he could not be a doctor for his own reasons, and his mother would still be thrilled. And it does not mean that she might have to say, "Look, Mom and Dad, what would really make *me* happy is the theater." It means that a young person must sit down and think, "Am I doing this for me, or for them, or to show them I'm right and they're wrong."

There are many family issues and values that affect career choices, such as salary, job satisfaction, and prestige. The family's experience with and response to initiative, advancement, hard work or the lack of it, workaholism, job dissatisfaction and self-employment versus working for someone else will have an effect on the young adult. It is by defining oneself in relationship to the values, issues, and experiences of one's family that one is able to choose what to bring to the next stage; the better one is able to separate one's issues and values from one's family the greater progress one will make in all the stages of the life cycle and the less chance there will be of reactively doing the opposite in an unsuccessful attempt to accomplish the separation process.

Until the women's movement of the late sixties, it had been somewhat more difficult for a woman to become her own person than for a man; many women skipped this stage altogether and were symbolically handed at the marriage ceremony from one man to another (from her father to her husband). The pervasive attitude was that a woman joined a man in marriage and helped him to complete *his* dream (such as supporting him through graduate school) so that he could get ahead in his career. Now women have their own dreams and career plans. This movement has created positive changes for women, but it is having repercussions on the family system. (This should not surprise us, since we know that every change in the system will have predictable chain reactions.) Some men feel threatened by women having a career and making more money than they do. Women also have to deal with their mothers and other women as they choose some of the more difficult options that are now available to them.

Intimacy with Peers. Intimacy is first learned and experienced in one's family of origin, where styles of emotional interaction are expressed by parents and learned, assimilated, modified, or reacted to by offspring. One of the tasks of young adulthood is to develop one-to-one relationships with peers of both sexes. Friendships take on deeper meaning as young people share interests and pastimes with others of their own age.

Romantic relationships and friendships with the opposite sex offer an opportunity to meet people whose backgrounds may be different. We have to learn how to communicate with others who are not privy to the same ways of communicating that we take for granted with family members. We have to teach others what we like and dislike, and they have to do the same for us. We may learn about our capacity for fun in one relationship and our need to talk intellectually about life in another.

In other words, relationships with peers continue the lifelong process of learning how to be close with others. Although a broken heart from an ill-fated romance is always painful, each person we are close to is another opportunity to learn about ourselves and others. I would not advocate promiscuity to young people, but dating a number of people before selecting a permanent partner is one of the wisest choices a young adult can make. What often happens is that the anxiety of separating from one's family of origin leads young people to choose a partner before they are fully separated from their parents.

To sum up this section: if a member of your family is about to enter the Unattached Young Adult phase, your concerns as a parent will be letting him or her go. If, for example, your child is having difficulty graduating from high school and moving on to college, it is wise to ask yourself at the same time if you are giving the child mixed messages about your willingness to let go. Or, if he or she is having trouble socially, are you too involved in this process—constantly making suggestions about how to attract boys, or what kind of girl is best for him? The task for the child is to finally grow up and make his or her own choices— for better or worse. Your task as a parent is to allow these choices to happen, giving advice when asked, and not offering "I told you so's" when things don't work out as planned.

If you are having trouble with this phase, you need to ask yourself "how come" and figure out what the payoff is for not moving on. Sometimes a young adult hesitates to move out of the house because he or she feels so needed by one or both parents that it would be quite a letdown to live alone or with a friend who was more self-sufficient.

If you had trouble with this phase in the past, you may still, in a later stage, be trying to cope with these tasks, as well as the tasks of the stage where you are right now. In fact, if you are a parent in the Launching Children stage and the issues here were not fully resolved, as is the case for many people, watching your children go through this time will create a good deal of discomfort for you.

The Joining of Families through Marriage—Stage 2

The shifting of primary loyalty from one's family of origin to the new spouse and marital system is one of the most difficult emotional transitions required during the life cycle. One reason for this is that many parents never teach their offspring that the new system that one is creating in marriage is supposed to take primary importance over the system that one has left. There are often many loyalty struggles around this issue, and it is normal to feel pulled, at times, between one's family of origin and one's spouse. The transition cannot be made overnight.

Becoming a Couple. As I said earlier, individuals occasionally choose spouses in an attempt to separate from their families of origin, and marriages formed for this reason get started on shaky ground. Indeed, most marital problems are the result of unresolved extended family problems (McGoldrick, 1980). The process of becoming a couple is difficult enough without one of the spouses constantly feeling that he/she is not No. 1. This problem hinders the development of intimacy since marital intimacy is effected by the ability of each adult to come to the relationship having separated from the emotional pulls and ties of the previous system.

A key issue—perhaps the key issue—is whom one decides to become a couple with. How far along we are in separating from our parents greatly affects this choice. Again, there are the options to marry the person that the family likes, or to marry the person the family hates, or to marry the person who truly meets our needs and hope that the rest of the family shares our joy.

The ritual of becoming a couple, the wedding, is often the

Figure 5-5

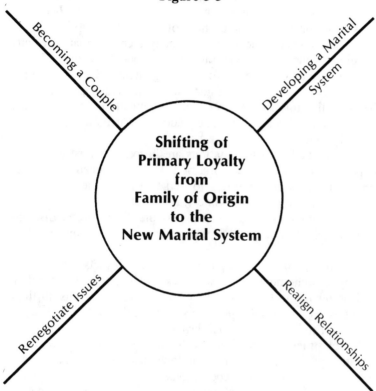

focus of much tension at this time. Mothers and daughters and the two families may be openly or quietly critical of the wedding plans, choices of attendants, etc. The triangle issue becomes the wedding itself, but the real issue is letting go of the primary loyalty.

Renegotiating Issues. The joining of two families brings together many traditions, values and issues to be renegotiated by the new couple. Each spouse may have only recently defined these values in the process of separating from his or her family of origin. Now each spouse will have to renegotiate some of those issues again. Such issues as spending holidays with family, money, career plans, and whether or not to have a child may have already been answered by the single adult and now must be renegotiated as a couple. Renegotiated does not necessarily mean changed; hopefully, these issues are not new but have been discussed during the courtship phase of the relationship.

As couples try to negotiate the many facets of marriage, any differences they managed to ignore, or considered intriguing in courtship, may become the focus of arguments. Even two people from similar backgrounds must face major changes when they begin to live together. Lesser issues—habits like not putting the toothpaste cap back on the tube—add to the irritations and stress of daily life.

Unfortunately, these irritations are in total contrast to the joy expected from being newly married. Having attained the love of one's life, it is disconcerting to find that he or she can also be annoying in the most picayune way. After the wedding is over and the honeymoon finished, many couples face extreme discomfort, which they may label incorrectly as having made a bad choice.

Depending on how their parents resolved conflicts in the family of origin, some newlyweds will seek distance from the problem and prefer not to talk about it, while others may focus all their energies on solving the problems of the relationship and begin to neglect their own personal development.

Development of the Marital System. People who marry in an attempt to fill up their own loneliness or emptiness enter marriage with enormous expectations about what the other spouse is going to do for them. Nobody could ever meet those expectations; when one spouse gets exhausted trying to meet those expectations and the other spouse gets angry because it is not enough, the marriage is under great stress.

When under stress, as we saw in Chapter 2, partners in the dyad tend to revert to one of two patterns, pursuit or distance. What happens, as the couple becomes a unit and negotiates responsibilities and ways to respond to each other emotionally that feel comfortable for both, is that a system, with its own unique patterns, is being formed.

A new set of chain reactions is set into motion, and chances are the balance of responsibility for various areas of family life is being more or less fixed. They are not necessarily fixed permanently, but they are becoming fixed until the family moves on or until one partner in the dyad decides a change must be made. In

114

other words, if the couple handles conflict by her refusing to speak with him until he apologizes in the first week, that pattern will still be with them in the 39th week, and in the 159th week, and so on. It will be fixed until he says, "Honey, this time I refuse to be the first to apologize." By this I don't mean that he's a victim who someday will rise and stand up for his rights, but that the couple establishes a ritual to handle arguments and that her not speaking and his apology are part of a ritual that will remain unchanged.

The roles of pursuer and distancer are generally assigned during this phase as well. Obviously there is no specific meeting on the topic; the pattern sets in and both agree to take on their respective roles silently. The couple learns by doing. If they are having difficulty establishing closeness at this stage, which many couples do, then the pattern of triangling to solve difficulties evolves or, in most cases, continues.

Realigning Relationships. Becoming a couple and the shifting of primary loyalty requires a realignment in the total relationship system of both spouses. This blending process is easier in some families than in others; some families have a tighter boundary around membership. It is the task of each spouse to try to make room for the new spouse in his/her system and the task of the other to try to join in those relationships. Each spouse not only has to deal with realigning parental relationships but must also renegotiate sibling, friend, and in-law relationships. For example, a close sibling relationship might be upset by a marriage, and that will need to be resolved in order for that sibling not to feel excluded from the new system.

If either spouse marries "to get out of the house," this task is apt to be extremely difficult. Friends too can exert a pull on one's loyalties. Many young couples may find themselves arguing about the time the other spends with friends. Friendship with members of the opposite sex is still another issue to be discussed, as well as finding other couples that both partners enjoy equally.

Some couples may go to an opposite extreme and focus too much attention on each other and the relationship. This "too much" is often a symptom of fusion; the couple is so close neither thinks of moving without the other. They may ignore friends who might be able to support them when they go through a bad time in the marriage. Or they may cut off family members who can also give them the special sort of love that only family can provide.

A couple's success in finding a good balance with relatives and friends is an important factor in later stages, as each family system needs the support of those outside the immediate family to function well.

If you are about to enter this phase or are newly married and experiencing difficulty, you can take comfort in knowing that you are not alone with this transition. Unfortunately, couples rarely come to therapy before marriage or in the early stages of marriage. For one thing, before marriage it is easier to ignore problems and after marriage and before children it is easier to get distance from the problems in outside activities.

If you are past this stage and are in a later stage involving children, try to look at the tasks discussed here for clues to present difficulties. How you solved, or did not solve, these issues with your spouse may be affecting your children now. As you try to cope with their specific problem (e.g., difficulty in school, finding friends, acting out), try to look at this stage of your married life for clues to how triangles may have started.

If your child is about to marry, you must face that you are going through a major loss. Your child's intended may be to your liking or not, and chances are there is little you can do about it at this point. The issue for you as you make plans for your child's wedding is to remember that with this very happy and beautiful occasion you will lose your child's official, primary loyalty. It may be what you want for him or her, but you are bound to have mixed feelings about it. If this is the case, it is wise to ask how these mixed feelings may be affecting your child and the plans for the big day.

The Family with Young Children—Stage 3

The central task facing the couple who has decided to have a child is to make room for that child in the family system. This not only means room in the physical sense of space in the home but also, and more importantly, in the emotional sphere of the existing relationship systems.

Making Room in the Marital System. The most difficult and most important adjustments take place in the marital system as

Figure 5-6

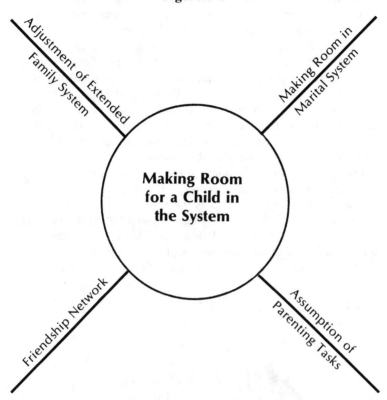

the two-person system becomes a threesome. The decision to have a child is a nodal event in the life of the couple and one that necessitates certain shifts which cause predictable emotional stresses for the couple. Even when both partners want to have a baby, share equally in the decision to have it, and try to anticipate and prepare themselves for the necessary shifts involved in adding a new member to the family, it is difficult. There are still predictable stresses for the couple to deal with.

The first threat to the marital dyad comes with the pregnancy. Two parents equally committed to the same choice have two totally different experiences during the pregnancy. She carries the child inside of her and experiences all the physical discomfort, as well as the first physical contact with the new child. He may easily feel neglected as she becomes too tired to enjoy things they once shared, or worried as he anticipates having more economic responsibilities. Since this is supposed to be another one of those happy times when we should all be experiencing nothing but pure joy, couples may often have difficulty sharing their different feelings about the event. Because the event is so big and can cause so much stress, the old patterns of distancing and pursuing come to the fore. If added to this is the stress of an unplanned child, or a child who was planned to take care of an already poor marital relationship, you can see why this time could be extremely uncomfortable for many couples.

The reality of making room for the developing baby becomes more apparent as the wife becomes more and more "pregnant," as illustrated in Figure 5-7. It is the task of the couple to make room for the new baby in the system without letting the baby get in the way of the marital relationship. This is easier said than done, but it is a crucial turning point, as failure to accomplish this task sets up numerous child-focused triangles.

Figure 5-7

The question of who is No. 1 often surfaces again as the baby takes on a vital and integral role in the family. It is perfectly normal for parents to feel resentful at times about the amount of time, space and energy that the baby now seems to be taking from the marital relationship. Likewise, it is also not unusual for either spouse to feel left out or neglected by all the attention that the baby receives from the other. These feelings need to be expressed and worked out so that the marital system can realign itself as a threesome.

In the case of adding a child, where the decision was made because one or both partners felt that something was missing in their relationship, this only adds more stress to a twosome that is already in distress. Adding a child as the remedy for a marital problem could be compared to building a triangle as a temporary solution to a much more serious and long-range problem.

Assumption of Parenting Tasks. The adjustments that are necessary as a couple tries to make room in the marital system for a child are not that easy and the difficulty of this transition is often made more stressful by the expectation that life with a new baby is supposed to be wonderful. The wife may want the husband to be an equal partner in baby care, or at least a very active participant, but often she feels that she knows more about how to hold, diaper and take care of a baby than her husband does. She may give the impression that there is only one right way to change a diaper (her way) and make the husband feel even more unsure of his child-care skills. He may then begin to back off and leave the job to the "expert," while she feels over-responsible for their baby.

In spite of many joys, the new parents find their marital relationship revolving around the baby's needs; there is less time to be together; and when there is time, one or both spouses are too exhausted to do more than collapse. With the new tasks of parenting added to the general pool of responsibilities, there is a need to renegotiate other responsibilities in light of the new family member's demands. While both parents may have worked before, the new mother may decide to stay home for a time or return to work part time. Does this mean she now cooks all the meals, when once they shared the chore? Or should he take over paying the bills, since his is the only check coming in?

Patterns of child-rearing learned in the family of origin may also cause conflict as they negotiate parenting tasks. He may have come from a family where it was good parenting to let the infant "cry it out," while no one in her family could stand the noise of a crying baby. Since the capabilities of young children and their needs change rapidly during the early years of development, these duties may have to be renegotiated continuously over time. For a year-old child, the question may be who is going to watch that he doesn't go in the street, while for a seven-year-old, the question may be who is going to volunteer to coach her local soccer team.

Patterns of overresponsibility and underresponsibility often emerge strongly here, as the lines between women's work and men's work are more firmly drawn for a while. The reality of raising kids and earning money may be dealt with in a variety of ways and the family's physical energies at this point are severely taxed.

Adjustment by Extended Family System. Well-meaning grandparents should not all of a sudden show up on the new parents' porch and say, "Well, we were in the area and thought that we'd stop by for a bit." Likewise, a new parent who was unable to separate appropriately before and set some realistic space between him/herself and the extended family should not use a child as an excuse to maintain distance. For example, "We can't come to visit because the baby needs a nap . . .," etc.

Another issue that some new parents have to address with their own parents is how their one-to-one relationship with each parent changes with the birth of a child. Some new parents feel that their parents or in-laws are no longer interested in visiting them, but come only to see the baby. Some very good "parent to young adult" relationships get shoved aside when a new baby enters the system; the task is to make room for the new baby, rather than allow the baby to take over the relationship system to the detriment of all others.

There are many situations where the decision to have a child is connected to an unresolved issue from either extended family and, as we discussed, these parents and children are prone to developing triangles in the new family system.

Friendship Network. The new couple has to make room in their social network to include their baby. This entails maintaining contact with friends who have children and with those who do not; sometimes this can become a dilemma when another couple is at a different life cycle stage than the one you are presently in; for example, this occurs when one couple is at the Family with Young Children stage while the other is at the Newly Married Couple stage.

Another major shift in the friendship network may occur if a wife leaves her career for a time to raise the baby and thus may not be able to maintain her relationship network with her friends at work; this could put additional stress on her as she tries to adjust to the new baby. With first babies, mothers often feel that they have to find a new network of friends that have babies around the same age in order not to feel isolated in their new role as "mother." This can be a difficult transition for a woman who leaves a career where she is comfortable, competent and surrounded by a cadre of friends and associates and takes on a new role where she has not, as yet, had a chance to develop expertise or a circle of close friends to support her.

Numerous triangles form throughout this stage of the family's life cycle because having a third person (a child) creates a fertile environment for the development of "child-focused" triangles. Likewise, "the more a couple centers on their children, the easier it is to avoid marital confrontation, because there is always something to worry, criticize, correct, or complain about with the children" (Barragan, 1976). The child-focused family is one that is developing and moving through the life cycle out of balance; something has gone wrong and the focus on the child is a compensation to attempt to alleviate another situation. For example, a woman who feels inadequate as a wife might overcompensate by attempting to become "super Mom," or a couple whose marriage is dull and boring might attempt to compensate by revolving their entire life around their children. In this latter case, one might wonder, if the topic of "children" was removed from this type of couple's conversation, would they ever have anything to talk about?

Children are often brought to therapists by their parents during this stage (during adolescence as well) and presented as the problem bearer (PB) in the family. This occurs because it is often easier to see the problem in someone else rather than to see one's own contribution to it and because parents find it easier to acknowledge having a problem child rather than a marital difficulty. This situation usually occurs with the child acting out or exhibiting symptomatic behavior that indicates that something is not going well. After careful study, one often finds that the symptomatic child is acting out some dysfunction existing in the family relationships. The fallout from these tensions increases the stress on the youngest or most vulnerable member in the family and the child's behavior is often an "S.O.S." for the family to get some help.

While it may be difficult to change the view that the child is the problem, and somehow his or her behavior needs modification, parents can try to take comfort in the fact that as adults they are more capable of making changes that will improve the family's functioning. Waiting for a child to see the light and make a move in a positive direction is a pretty frustrating position to be in.

Unfortunately, facing difficulties in the marriage brings up the threatening topic of divorce, and families with young children may shy away from direct confrontation, with good reason. If both parents can face that not being happy with the status quo requires change and accept that change will not be easy but will be worthwhile, the family in this stage can face difficulties with more security. The fact is that the longer major difficulties progress the more likelihood there is that somewhere along the line a family member—child, parent, even grandchild—is going to suffer severely for the entire system's failure to work out problems.

Couples without children continue to work on the tasks of the first two stages—skipping the stages and tasks of the Family with Young Children, Family with Adolescents, and Launching Children and Moving On—and, at an age-appropriate time, move into the Family in Later Life stage. There are an increasing number of couples who are choosing not to have children; the impact of this decision on the life cycle processes is not yet fully known because not enough couples at this time have chosen to remain childless in order for this decision to be studied over a long enough period of time.

The Family with Adolescents—Stage 4

Adolescence is often a stormy time for families. One of the major reasons for this is that the adolescent begins in earnest the crucial task of separating from his/her family of origin. Few adolescents know how to cope with the various pulls they are feeling and many parents have difficulty with their chief task of this period, namely, flexibility in both setting limits and letting go. There is a mutual process of giving and taking by both parents and adolescents to help the adolescent attain freedom with responsibility.

It is a very delicate balance which is not easy to strike because every adolescent is unique; two adolescents from the same family may begin this process at very different times and progress through it at different rates. Likewise, parents may not be able to let go or set firm limits with an adolescent because of some issue that they are struggling with themselves.

Figure 5-8

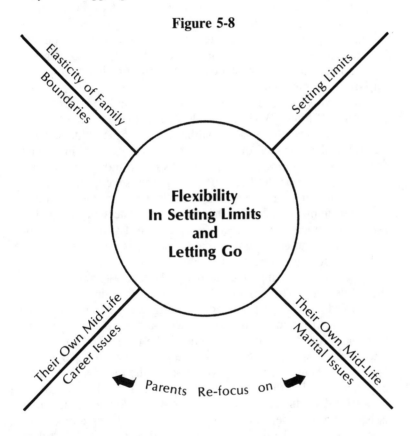

Elasticity of Family Boundaries. Parents have the enormously difficult task of preparing their offspring to become independent and to leave them; they are expected to love and take care of their child in such a way that the child is able to leave them freely without feeling that there are strings attached. Parents need to ask themselves whether or not they raise children so that the children will take care of them later on or so that the children will be able to leave home and have a life of their own.

The confusion of dealing with adolescents is that one day they need you and the next they don't. There is a constant back-and-forth struggle within themselves for independence. For weeks your youngster might play records in his room and then emerge and try to get very involved in some project to fix up the house. When the adolescent chooses distance, as many do at this stage to handle separation, it is difficult to know how much to pursue him or her. There is a fine line between leaving the adolescent feeling neglected and constantly nagging him or her to join you on family outings, etc.

Friendships become extremely important and romances may begin in full force. When the adolescent is experiencing "puppy love," Mom, Dad and younger siblings may be the ultimate drag, but when the romance dies he or she may come running home for shelter. When their friends start spending more time around the house, one may find oneself coping with several more adult-sized bodies. It's one thing to have little playmates outside in the yard and another to have a bunch of six-footers in one of the family bedrooms playing records. And then if your house is not the hangout, the complaint is that he or she is never home.

Doing the right thing by an adolescent is exceedingly difficult because the right thing changes daily. This is not to poke fun at the adolescent. The emotional struggle of this time cannot be minimized—fears of attractiveness, being accepted, getting good grades, facing a future on one's own—are enormous. Anyone who has been divorced can vouch for the pain of facing again, after a long respite, the issue of one's attractiveness to the opposite sex. Adolescents themselves worry about the mood swings they experience and do not need that to become a family joke.

Setting Limits. The correct balance of freedom and limits that is necessary in order to develop a responsible young adult is not easy to strike and this is why the tug-of-war is so stressful at times. When is the adolescent ready for this freedom and responsibility and when is there still a need for limits?

Adolescents try to assert their independence and separateness in many different ways. One common characteristic of this attempt is the degree to which they vacillate on so many things. They can see you, as a parent, being wonderful one minute and positively awful the next; one day your ideas make sense and the next you know nothing. The adolescent also exhibits wide swings in regard to mood, degree of responsibility, and attitude toward family values, rules and traditions. Adolescents will often test, attack or discard some parental values as part of their way of establishing their own values and identity. When this happens it is very important for parents not to change their values, but to be firm and make their values known, stating clearly what expectations they have about the adolescent's behavior while living in their home.

The setting of limits is crucial during the adolescent stage. Since this period is seen as a major thrust by the adolescent to separate from his/her family, it is important that the adolescent have something to move away or break away from. If parents keep changing their values, rules, and positions on issues because of resistance or uproar from their adolescent, they will not be helping their child find his/her own value system but rather will be confusing him/her more. This does not mean that rules should be laid down in cement but that parents need to be both firm and flexible in handling their adolescent. A firm yet flexible position is more difficult to maintain because it calls for more judgment than if one adopts a rigid or laissez-faire position. It is fine to compromise and negotiate on certain reasonable issues; that is where flexibility comes in.

Using the analogy of the family as a sailboat, adolescence can be seen as a very stormy time in which the boat will be rocked, water will come roaring in over the sides, lightning will strike and the course may need to be adjusted to avoid rocks and shoals, but hopefully the boat will neither capsize nor lose its direction. If the captains (the parents) do not hold a firm course through these turbulent waters, the surges of adolescence will throw the boat and all its crew off course.

Let's talk about the "captains" for a moment. There has to be agreement when trying to steer a course; you can't sail North for a while and then South for a while and hope to get anywhere. This is often what happens when parents are not communicating well while trying to navigate the turbulent waters of adolescence. When parents are unable to agree on how to manage their adolescent, the entire family is in for trouble. Adolescents will always play their parents off against each other where possible; this sets up a natural triangle if the parents allow it.

Parental Issues in Adolescence. (a) *Marriage/Adolescent Sexuality.* During the turmoil of adolescence, it is easy for parents to lose sight of their tasks, which are to focus on their own mid-life marital and career issues. It would be so much simpler for a couple to try to shape up their adolescent than to take a serious look at where the marital relationship is. We know from systems theory how one issue in a family can affect everyone and that chain reactions can easily be set off. There are several points in the life cycle in which both the parents and the adolescent simultaneously face the same potent issue, and the intersection of those attempts intensifies and complicates their relationship.

Sexuality is one of the most potent issues of adolescence, and the teenager's development can trigger an unresolved parental issue, thus making it extremely difficult for the parents to deal constructively with the adolescent. Likewise, when the adolescent is faced with this issue and knows his/her parents had trouble with it, the adolescent is sometimes prone to deal reactively with the situation by doing the opposite. A child with very religious parents, who valued virginity, could act out sexually. And a child who knows his or her parents "had to get married" may veer away from dating altogether.

Some couples with teenagers unfortunately describe their own sexual interaction as being routine, infrequent, and not what it could be; even discussing it provokes an argument. The intersection of this parental problem with an adolescent's budding sexuality intensifies the conflict. The parents may overfocus in a rigid fashion on their adolescent's normal sexual development and curiosity as a way of not dealing with their own sexual issues. In addition, the adolescent, in tune with his/her own growing sexuality, may add fuel to the fire by flaunting it in front of his/her parents almost as if to say, "What is the matter with you guys . . . you don't even touch or kiss anymore?"

(b) *Career Success/Adolescent Academic Performance.* This is another common area in which parents with unresolved issues about a career or the lack thereof can put undue pressure on their children. A father who is feeling unsuccessful about his career achievements could overreact to his son's performance at school; or a mother might pressure her daughter to have a career because she never had one. In both of these cases the parents might mean well but their own unresolved feelings cause them to overreact to their child, probably producing negative results. The flip side of this situation is the adolescent who looks at the successful career path of the parent(s) and the price tag paid for it and says, "No way am I going to kill myself like that . . . it isn't worth it!" Then you are off and running into another type of battle.

The adolescent needs to begin thinking about a career choice and what steps are necessary in order to pursue that career path. This usually involves becoming attached to other adults as role models, such as teachers, coaches, or even heroes in the world of sports or popular music. These tasks begin during this stage for adolescents and are continued in greater depth in the "Unattached Young Adult" stage which follows for them. Although both parents and adolescents need to be doing their part in negotiating this stage, I emphasize the tasks that parents need to be accomplishing because the greatest power and ability to make things work in a family rests with the parents, since they are the adults and more mature members of the family. If the parents have their "act" together, the entire family has a better chance of successfully accomplishing the tasks of this stage.

Summary. Adolescence can be seen as a bridge or connector between the traditions of the past and what will happen in the future. It is a time of new ideas, causes and movements that vibrate through the family—a time when the older generation cringes at hair styles, music and dress, hoping that it will pass. It is often a period where the pendulum swings far to one side before it returns to a more moderate course in young adulthood.

One important way for parents to help their adolescent negotiate the turmoil of adolescence is to stay "self-focused" on their own tasks. The fewer unresolved issues they are facing the better able they will be to objectively help their adolescent negotiate this stage. Likewise, it is crucial for the adolescent not to get him/herself enmeshed in his parents' unresolved issues. The older adolescent who should be preparing to leave home sometimes allows him/herself to get caught in the position of trying to make one last attempt to help the parents come together. This attempt frequently surfaces in acting-out behavior which gives the parents a common or mutual goal to focus their interaction around.

In such cases, the adolescent who appears to be innocently sacrificing himself or herself has to take a close look at what he/she is doing because in a family system there are no innocent

Figure 5-9

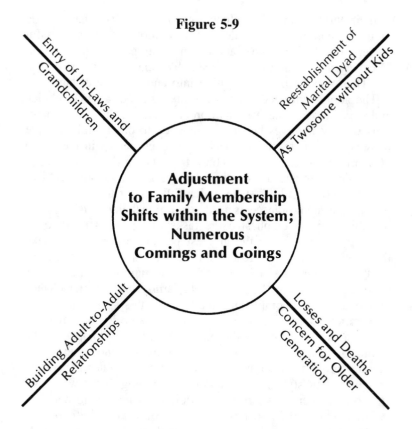

Entry of In-Laws and Grandchildren

Reestablishment of Marital Dyad As Twosome without Kids

Adjustment to Family Membership Shifts within the System; Numerous Comings and Goings

Building Adult-to-Adult Relationships

Losses and Deaths Concern for Older Generation

victims; everyone plays a part in the problem. What part is this adolescent playing in this dysfunctional triangle? Is the adolescent not ready to leave home and, therefore, will the acting-out behavior in school prevent his/her graduation and allow him/her to remain in the security of the home instead of moving on? Or does the adolescent love the attention, even though it is negative, that his/her disruptive behavior creates? Is this the only way he/she can be noticed and feel important? This common "child-focused" triangle has three people who are all involved and collaborating in a dysfunctional pattern.

It is important during the swings of this stage not to "throw the baby out with the bath water," that is, not to throw away a good relationship that has been developing over fifteen years because the adolescent wants his or her hair or music a certain way or because he or she makes one mistake and gets in some trouble. Adolescence is a time of troubles, but families can turn mistakes into learning experiences rather than into broken relationships.

Launching Children and Moving On—Stage 5

Both parents and young adults face crucial tasks during this stage. Parents first have the task of supporting and encouraging their children in moving out of the home, both physically and emotionally (launching), and then the parents must go on to reestablish their marital relationship as a twosome without children at home. The children have the task of developing greater independence and autonomy as they separate from their family of origin and enter "The Unattached Young Adult" stage.

Reestablishment of Marital Dyad. The "Launching Children and Moving On" stage is being greatly affected by the decrease in the birth rate and the increased life expectancy of parents. These factors have extended the length of time couples spend in this stage because there are fewer children to raise and launch and, consequently, more years together without children at home before reaching retirement age and entrance into the "Later Life" stage. In the past, couples had child-rearing responsibilities as a primary focus for a much longer time; but now, as many couples become a twosome at a much earlier age, some are finding this transition difficult because they allowed the raising of children to become more important than the marriage. The task of returning to being a twosome obviously cannot be accomplished until after all of the children have been launched. This is exactly where some couples get stuck.

During this stage in the family life cycle, the husband often sees the exodus of the kids as his chance to slow down at the office, take a little more vacation, and even think about retirement; the opposite may be occurring for his wife. If she had a career, she may have had it interrupted or slowed down by her children and may be just about back on her career course. Likewise, she may just be beginning a career and enjoying the excitement of it. There is no easy solution to these potential conflicts; but awareness of the issues and talking about them when they develop can ease the transition and reduce stress.

When a family gets stuck in the launching process, it is never any one person's fault. Everyone plays a part; parents have trouble in letting go and children have trouble in leaving. Another symptom of this problem is often seen when a student fails to get his/her college applications completed. As this unfolds, one learns that the adolescent has gotten him/herself enmeshed in balancing out the marital relationship and fears that if he/she leaves, the marriage will experience turmoil. There is, of course, the possibility of that occurring, but there is also the possibility that parents will successfully deal with the problem between themselves when there is no longer a buffer.

Let us not assume in this case that the adolescent is an innocent victim prevented by his/her parents from filling out the college applications; somehow this behavior is serving a purpose for him/her. For example, he/she may not want to give up the special and powerful role that he/she plays in the life of both parents as their personal marriage counselor. This is another example of how everyone's behavior must be understood in the context of the family system.

Building Adult-to-Adult Relationships. This brings us to the goal of changing the parent-child relationship, which is impossible as long as you are supporting the young adult under your roof and treating him/her as a dependent. Some parents and young adults find this to be a difficult relationship shift. Some difficulty is predictable since the relationship has been parent-child for so long; but if it is allowed to persist it will hinder the separation process and transitions to later stages.

In spite of the fact that this stage is often referred to as the time of the "empty nest," there are an increasing number of young people who have returned to the nest over the last several years for a variety of reasons, including the economy, job loss, graduation from school and not yet employed, marital separation and/or divorce. When the prospect comes up of having a launched young adult return home, there should always be a good reason and a re-launching plan established before a young adult is allowed to return home. Allowing a young adult to return home is not a question of loving him/her more or less, but rather loving him/her enough to make sure that coming home is the best option. When returning home always appears to be the best choice, the chances are good that separation hasn't yet occurred.

When the parents decide that the best choice is to allow the young adult to return home because it is best for him/her, rather than because it would make things better between the parents, then there should be a plan devised by the parents and the young adult about how to get him/her re-launched. For example, a young adult might be told: you may live here for a defined period of time, you must contribute to the house financially and help out with the chores, and there are certain rules that we expect you to follow while living in our home. The plan is constructed to re-launch the young adult, which is a mutual task at this point.

Entry of In-laws and Grandchildren. Also during this stage, parents are asked to become increasingly flexible in the comings and goings of their children as they are being launched. For example, a son visits for one day and is gone the next. You meet his girlfriend, try to get to know her, only to find by his next visit that she has been replaced. Family boundaries are again tested for their elasticity as parents are asked during this stage to accept and make room for the marriage partners and the in-laws that their children choose. Here is where parents must face the shift of their child's loyalty. There is no need to deny the loss felt when there's a missing place at the dinner table on a holiday. However, it is important to accept that your loss coexists with your child's happiness.

Concern for the Older Generation. Couples can anticipate in this stage a growing awareness and concern for the older generation. Loved ones will be dying and close friends may become ill and infirm. Couples who have successfully launched their children and paid off the college loans may now be finding their aged parents asking them for either financial or emotional support. How to assist them to meet their needs while encouraging their autonomy in the coming years will be a major issue.

One point to keep in mind is that taking in an aging parent need not be the only option. Some people feel an overwhelming need to take in their parents out of obligation or guilt but then treat them miserably out of resentment. Older people should be encouraged and supported to be independent just as they taught their children to be growing up. Respecting their dignity and ablility to take care of themselves is important; they have been used to their own space and it is often better not to do for them what they are able to do themselves.

These pending losses of parents and the reality of dealing with their illness can stir up ancient sibling rivalries and resentments. The child who long ago chose to live near his or her parents may now feel overresponsible for their care in relation to siblings across country. Since many of us find it difficult to speak openly about such issues, the resentments that build can put an added emotional strain on the situation. However, on the other hand, being angry with a brother for not doing his fair share can also be a convenient cover-up for the real issue, facing the death of the people who brought you into the world.

This stage may also bring up the question of adding a parent to the household. This is a very personal decision, as individual as deciding to add another child to the household. People need to consider all the options available to them and ideally be able to discuss the issue with the parent in question. A majority of older people would prefer to live in their own homes, and other ways of supporting them are becoming increasingly available.

If the decision to take the parent into the household is made, the couple needs to be prepared to make a major adjustment. Depending on the relationship between the parent and the child in the family of origin, this transition may be more or less smooth. In any case, it is best if the couple makes adequate provisions to preserve the marital dyad.

The Family in Later Life—Stage 6

People can generally be said to enter "The Family in Later Life" stage around the age of sixty-five and, as Figure 5-10 clearly points out, there are enormous tasks to be tackled in this stage. It is probably the stage that we know the least about because most of us are not there yet, nor are we rushing to get there; likewise, we do not want to find out more about this stage until we finally have to face it. In spite of this reluctance, it is still important to understand the implications of the issues described in Figure 5-10 so that we will be better prepared to deal with the stresses of this period.

Maintaining Emotional and Physical Well-Being. Health care and sickness are major concerns to the individuals in the "Later Life" stage and to their offspring. Like so many issues throughout the life cycle, health care involves mutual and

Figure 5-10

Maintaining Emotional and Physical Well-Being

Retirement

**Adjustment
to Shifting
Generational
Roles**

Staying Connected to Younger Generation

Loss of Spouse and Sibling

reciprocal interplay between both generations. The individual in the "Later Life" stage has the task of striving to maintain his/her physical and emotional well-being as best as he/she can while trying to maintain as much autonomy and independence as possible. Adult children often have concerns about how best to help their aging parents face physiological decline and worry about how to strike the proper balance of supporting the older generation while at the same time neither overfunctioning for them nor taking away their autonomy.

Loss of Spouse and Siblings. Another major concern is how to adjust to the death of a spouse. Women are four times as likely as men to become widows and more likely to be widowed at an earlier age with many years of life ahead (Walsh, 1980). These

133

anxieties begin for women long before they enter the "Later Life" stage, and their intensity increases as the possibility of widowhood becomes more and more of a reality. Both men and women need to be prepared both psychologically and financially for this eventuality. Men who become widowers often find it more difficult to adjust to the death of their spouses than do widows because men generally do not anticipate outliving their wives and thus having to deal with thoughts of living alone. They have also often counted on their wives to be in charge of their relationship networks. Without their wives, they may feel isolated and fail to use their social skills to reach out and to reestablish connections with family and friends.

Retirement. Retirement can be another stumbling block for some couples. They have never had as much time alone together as they do now, and this takes time and effort to adjust to. It is unfortunate that couples have so much more time together in retirement when resources and energy are in decline rather that at earlier points in their lives. Retirement is also a time when the man becomes assimilated into what is often the woman's domain in the household. This is changing somewhat now because with more married women in the workforce it is very likely that more couples will be retiring around the same time with both having to get used to being in the house together for longer hours.

Staying Connected to Children and Grandchildren. There is often much pessimistic talk about old age and the way people are treated by their families as they get older. If families have been working on maintaining viable generational connectors, there need not be any reason for pessimistic thinking. It is when the connectors break down that the potential for loneliness and isolation sets in. There is so much that the older generation can contribute if one can just listen and make use of their wisdom and experience.

The lengthy case history that follows shows how problems generated in one stage of the family life cycle can mushroom at a later stage. Figure 5-11 is a genogram of this family.

Michael Brown, 28, came to the initial therapy session with his mother, Lucy Brown, 52. Michael's visit was part of a plea-bargaining decision that had been arranged after Michael was arrested for drunk driving. The judge required that Michael seek

Figure 5-11

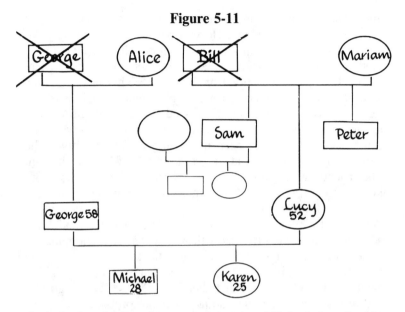

alcohol education, and suggested therapy. Michael described his basic drinking pattern as "two or three beers a day," but said he also liked to "get loaded" from time to time. His arrest had followed the bachelor party of an old friend.

Michael was still living at home with his parents and was reluctantly working for his father in the plumbing supply business started by his grandfather. When questioned at first, Lucy said she hadn't minded her son living at home, except that she feared he would "burn the house down" because he smoked. Michael had always enjoyed drinking and parties, but these habits had been saved for outside the home until the last two years. Michael's girlfriend at the time broke up with him because he refused to get engaged. Shortly thereafter she met a somewhat older man who, Michael said, had "a lot of money," and married him. Michael deeply regretted that he had not moved to marry this young woman and began to stay home more. Also, at this time, many of his friends had already married and some had children, which gave him fewer companions.

Michael, a young man in the Unattached Young Adult Stage, was clearly having trouble with all the major tasks of this stage. He was still living at home, was working in a job he didn't like which was part of the family business, and was virtually cut off from contact with his peers. He was becoming increasingly depressed, and often sat up into the night watching television by himself and smoking cigarettes, as his mother complained. There was practically no separation from his parents whatsoever, despite the fact that Michael had been a seemingly gregarious adolescent.

Lucy Brown was also very distressed at this point in time. For the past sixteen years she had worked for a small local advertising agency and had recently been made an account executive. She admitted to the therapist that she was ashamed of Michael in front of her friends at the office and was disappointed he was not more like his sister Karen, 25. When questioned about her marriage, Lucy said, "I don't interfere in George's business and he doesn't interfere with mine." The couple did little together, and Lucy had two close women friends with whom she went shopping, to movies and museums. Lucy's mother Marian had recently been found to have stomach cancer, a fact that was also weighing heavily on Lucy's mind. Her father Bill died two years ago of a heart attack. She listed her son as her major problem, however. Her lack of closeness with her husband she claimed to have accepted many years before. Her mother's pending death she viewed as "a fact of life."

Michael said he had thought of "getting help," but had never felt bad enough to do so. He was relieved that the judge had referred him to therapy. Since his breakup with his girlfriend, he had really not been close to anyone. He listed his goals as moving out of the house and getting a different job so that he would meet more people his own age. He was afraid to let down his father, who had repeatedly told him as a child, "The only reason I kill myself at this job, Son, is so that someday it will be yours."

George Brown, 58, came to the second session at the request of the therapist. When asked what he thought the problems of the family were, he said that he was severely disappointed in Michael because he had let the business decline in the past two years. At that time George had gone into semiretirement and began to work only four days a week. His own father had a premature heart attack at age 44 and George was beginning to feel his own decline. After working 60 to 70 hours a week all his life, he felt he wanted to enjoy himself. He had belatedly taken up golf and was pleased with his progress in the sport.

136

He talked frequently about moving to Florida, but Lucy strenuously objected. George also felt responsible for his aging mother, who had made a poor adjustment to widowhood. George was an only child and, although his mother Alice was in good health, she had not developed friendships with people her own age. George did all the maintenance on both houses, and had suggested to Lucy that it would be easier for him if Alice moved in with them. He jokingly described himself as "torn between two women." George was having his own trouble with the Launching Children Stage. He finally wanted to move closer to his wife, which was a major reason why he suggested moving to Florida, and hoped she would take up golf as well. He felt his son and his mother were his major obstacles.

Karen was recently graduated from Georgetown Law School and was working in Washington, D.C., for a congressman. At the request of her mother, Karen joined the family for a session and later came for a private interview. Karen was the family "star." Her mother bragged about her daughter's accomplishments and all the young men Karen was dating. George said he wished Karen had shown an interest in the business because she might do a better job than her brother. Even Michael described Karen as his "favorite" person in the family. During the session, Karen expressed her concern for "all of them," particularly Michael. She was actually quite maternal toward her older brother, and the two did get along well. Alone, Karen spoke frankly with the therapist about her need to live at a distance so she would not get "sucked in" to the family's problems. She described her parents' marriage as a "cold war" and felt sorry for her brother's predicament. She spoke defiantly that a "woman must be able to make it without a man," and her current pattern was one of having several relationships going on at once so as not to get "too close." She bragged that she had never been "in love." Her strong guilt and fears about being involved with men indicate that, although she may have been well separated from her family in her career choice, in the other two areas of this stage she was having as much trouble as her brother. Even her career choice could be questioned as a reaction against men and love, rather than a choice to be a lawyer.

In this Launching Children phase, the therapist saw a number of triangles, including: George, Lucy and Michael; George, Lucy

137

and Alice; George, Lucy and Lucy's women friends; George, Michael and the family business; the "family," Karen, Karen's job. In fact, it was safe to say that every member of the family was involved in numerous combinations of triangles, all of which were interlocking.

The background gathered about the Adolescent stage was not surprising. Ten years ago, as a teenager, Michael had been a "good-time kid," according to his father. Popular in school, he was never a student. His mother reportedly wanted him to go to college, but continually nagged him on the subject because she viewed him as a "hopeless case" in the school department. Michael reasoned that since he was only going into the family business, there was no sense in "wasting time studying." Besides, he felt it was useless to try to outshine his sister in academics. At that stage of development he liked being out with his friends, driving his old car, going to parties and, when home, listening to music in his room.

Karen recalled intense pressure from her mother to perform well in school. Her mother's words were "a woman without money is chained to a man." Her good grades were "expected" by both parents, and most of her conversations with her mother concerned the older woman's concern for Michael. Karen studied four to six hours a night in high school, but said she constantly worried about how well she was doing. She was totally amazed to have been selected valedictorian. She subsequently went to Boston College and graduated *magna cum laude*.

Lucy constantly pursued Michael about his grades, comparing him unfavorably to his sister and the children of their friends. George was unconcerned about Michael for the most part, especially because he had been a "wild kid" himself. He was proud that Michael was "sowing his oats." As Michael got older, George saw the service as the answer to his immaturity. George felt that World War II had made a man out of him and that Michael would benefit from enlisting. Lucy disagreed. With Karen, George was extremely protective and strict about curfews and companions. He did not want Karen to be "available" to boys like Michael. Karen was very compliant during high school, but once away at college became sexually active, to the point of being promiscuous.

Michael had a couple of steady girlfriends in high school and became sexually active at 16. He went steady with one young woman from the age of 17 until 20, when she broke up with him because he did not want to get married. When he met the young woman he had been thinking of going to California, but had stayed because of the relationship. Again, he repeated his pattern of putting all his attention on one young woman, but refusing to make a commitment.

When her children became teenagers, Lucy announced that her family "no longer needed her" and began her career in earnest. She also cultivated female friends. George became obsessed with what Karen's education was going to cost and kept saying, "Thank God Michael won't be going to college" from the time the boy was 12. He started to work as many as seven days a week. The family business was also the sole support of Alice, since George, Sr., had died when Michael was 11 and Karen was 8. Lucy resented the drain on the family income and further justified her work by saying that "one income doesn't cover two houses." As teenagers, Michael and Karen were a close sibling pair and when her mother was out Karen cooked for Michael. Michael joined George in protecting Karen from boys her own age.

In the Adolescent stage, the Browns were involved with all the usual difficulties. What was immediately obvious was that everyone had labeled Karen "the student" and Michael "the ne'er-do-well." Lucy was taking a long-awaited step toward a career, but her statement about "not being needed" smacked of reacting *against* her children's leaving and not *for* herself. George was feeling overburdened economically, but was threatened by the idea that his wife "had to work." He was having difficulty letting go of Karen, seemed disinterested in his wife and Michael and felt overresponsible for his own mother.

Going back one stage further into the Family with Young Children stage, both Lucy and George reported that Michael had been a "hellion," and that Karen had been extremely bright. Notably, Michael was not named George, as Alice and George, Sr., expected he would be. This slight to George's parents was something Lucy was proud at having been able to accomplish. Lucy said she always felt George was too involved with his mother and "his family business," and that the early childhood years, her thirties, had been the most miserable years of her life. She regretted not having a career, as her own mother had wanted her to do, but at the same time followed the path of the grandmothers in staying home with her children. She said George had never held the children when they were infants, nor did he participate in their routine care. Her mother helped out by sitting one afternoon a week, but didn't like to leave her father to sit for the young couple at night. Besides, back then, she said, George was often too tired to go out and all he wanted to do was watch TV. Lucy said that when they were children she had to "do everything" for Michael, while Karen was self-sufficient from an early age. She resented Michael for this, but thought it was part of the difference between boys and girls.

Again, from what we know about triangles, one can see that there were numerous triangles at work in this family for many years. The frustrations of an earlier time could easily be linked to the present situation where Michael was apparently unable to leave home. He was still living out the legacy of a "hellion" and the boy who couldn't "do anything" for himself. Throughout childhood, the distance between the parents was always closed by Michael's misbehavior. While this misbehavior never reached drastic proportions during childhood, as a young adult it was finally seriously hampering Michael's happiness and independence. And while everyone was pointing at Michael as the "family problem," each obviously had his or her share of personal conflict over some family issue.

Since Michael was having such difficulty with this stage, the therapist also wanted to know how George and Lucy handled the Unattached Young Adult phase and the New Couple stage. George's leaving home had been initiated by the war, and afterward he had returned home to attend a nearby college. His own father was a forceful man who dominated the family when he was home, but generally left Alice and George to themselves as he put his focus on the business. George's "wild days" were brought to a close by his marriage to Lucy. However, like Michael, he did not have extensive dating experience before settling down with Lucy.

As a young boy, George was his mother's confidant. His parents' style of arguing was to maintain many days of silence, during which both would speak only to him. In his new marriage George also adopted the "silent treatment" as the best way to solve differences. Lucy's parents had a volatile relationship, which included some physical violence. In the marriage Lucy had been anxious to keep peace for herself and for her children because she knew how terrified she was when her own parents fought. In George's parents' marriage his mother had also resented the business, but still wanted her son to become a part of it. In the present nuclear family, Karen was her mother's confidante, but Michael was still able to draw both parents' attention with misbehavior.

Unlike Alice, Lucy did not want her son to go into the family business, but she felt his poor school performance left him no other choice. This lack of confidence in men was a pattern from Lucy's family of origin. Lucy's older brother Sam left home at an early age, married and had children right away. He was financially unsuccessful, as was her younger brother Peter who never left home. Lucy was her mother's pride and joy and had been the only child to attend college. She had worked for an advertising agency in New York City, commuting from her home in Connecticut, but had been unable to move into the city because she hesitated to leave her brother Peter alone at home. Like Michael and Karen, the brother and sister were extremely close. However, when she met and fell in love with George, she felt justified in leaving home. She married and worked until she became visibly pregnant with Michael a year and a half later. Lucy reported that she actually got pregnant to "drag George away from his mother." As we can see, both George and Lucy and Lucy's brothers had difficulty with the Unattached Young Adult phase, and George and Lucy had difficulty with the New Couple phase. This spilled over into the Family with Young Children phase, as the choice to have children was partly a reaction against Alice, rather than a decision "for" having children. We see patterns of one generation mirrored in the patterns of the next, as well as reactions against old patterns.

Michael and Lucy proved to be the most willing participants in therapy. Karen was cooperative but distance kept her out of the process. She did, however, seek therapy in Washington. Lucy's motivation was strong because now that her mother was dying she worried that Michael might end up alone, as her brother Peter would be soon. The therapy focused on Michael, with Lucy and George occasionally coming for sessions with their grown son.

Michael started with a process of settling career issues and

141

confronting his father with their differences. He discovered for himself that he actually liked the business better than his father did, but that, since he had felt second-best to Karen, it had always seemed like a second-rate choice. This bad label he inherited kept him from putting himself into the work. Once he found this out, he applied himself to learning the business and making suggestions for change. Within a year, business had improved and Michael had moved to his own apartment. He was dating a young woman who lived in the same building. George had hired out the household maintenance on his mother's house and asked Lucy to spend more time with him. The couple had even played golf together, although Lucy said she preferred the movies. Even Alice, who never participated in a session, felt the impact of the changes and joined a local senior citizens group.

Certainly, the death of Lucy's mother will again disrupt this family's balance, as would a decision on Michael's part to marry his girlfriend. It would also be interesting to see how Karen resolves the issue of intimate relationships with men. However, through the therapy process, all members had been able to re-work their respective stages of life cycle development and were ready to face the next step with more strength than they had previously had.

Divorce and the Family Life Cycle

Before concluding this section, we need to consider briefly a major disruptive event occurring in many families at some point in the life cycle, namely, divorce. Families who experience a divorce go through significant upset and disruption to their life cycle; the family and its members will have an additional stressful period or cycle to go through in order to reestablish optimal family movement through the rest of the life cycle. Figure 5-12 depicts the life course of two families where one family has experienced the additional stress of a divorce.

In the course of the journey through the life cycle, Family A had to deal with the emotional upset of divorce between 1977 and 1979; however, the outcome of that divorce may have left that family in a much better place than before to continue the process toward healthy family functioning. It would be incorrect, therefore, to assume that the level of functioning in 1981 is better

Figure 5-12

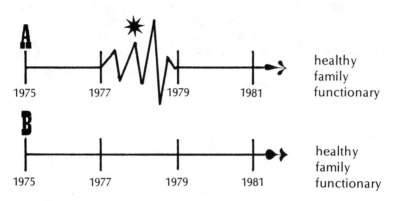

in Family B than in Family A just because Family B did not experience a divorce. Comparing levels of functioning between families is unproductive; however, it is important to note that Family A faced additional developmental tasks (as indicated by an asterisk *) due to the divorce. Some of these tasks were for the mother and father to work to achieve not only a physical divorce but also an emotional divorce, for the mother and father to maintain post-divorce contact that allows for the co-parenting of their children, and for the children to establish one-to-one relationships with each parent, to work through the loyalty struggles that they will experience, and to avoid taking sides in their parents' disputes. These are only a few of the additional issues that a divorcing family has to face in addition to all the other normal tasks of each life cycle stage. There are other issues to be dealt with should either of the spouses decide to remarry.

Divorce, in some cases, could be the most effective way to promote the growth of each spouse and also produce healthy children. It is certainly far from healthy for spouses to be in constant warfare with each other, with the "fallout" of each battle landing on the kids. However, divorce too often fails to end the battles and frequently produces long cold wars. This type of divorce never leads to the resumption of healthy family functioning but rather tends to impede the growth of all family members. It is the difficult task of divorcing parents to try to promote the future growth of the other spouse (your child's other parent) so that the outcome of the emotional turmoil brought about by a divorce leaves the spouses as whole and integrated people capable of co-parenting their children, separately and effectively. This goal is often lost sight of as the divorcing spouses enter the volatile legal arena; but it is certainly a principle that would lead to healthier family functioning after divorce.

References

Mariano Barragan, "The Child-Centered Family," in *Family Therapy: Theory and Practice,* ed. Philip J. Guerin, Jr. (New York: Gardner Press, Inc., 1976).

E. A. Carter and M. McGoldrick, *The Family Life Cycle: A Framework for Family Therapy* (New York: Gardner Press, Inc., 1980).

Daniel J. Levinson, *The Seasons of a Man's Life* (New York: Ballantine Books, 1978).

Theodore Lidz, *The Person* (New York: Basic Books, 1968).

M. McGoldrick, "The Joining of Families through Marriage: The New Couple," in *The Family Life Cycle: A Framework for Family Therapy,* ed. E. A. Carter and M. McGoldrick (New York: Gardner Press, Inc., 1980).

Gail Sheehy, *Passages* (New York: Bantam Books, Inc., 1974).

Froma Walsh, "The Family in Later Life," in *The Family Life Cycle: A Framework for Family Therapy,* ed. E. A. Carter and M. McGoldrick (New York: Gardner Press, Inc., 1980).

CHAPTER SIX

The Change Process

THROUGHOUT this book I have been talking about patterns, balance, goals of family life, and places where families may get into trouble. As a family consultant, I tell families that when things are going well they should leave well enough alone and enjoy it; but, when the family stress is too high or when one family member's stress is too high and everyone else is complaining about his or her problem, change is important. Let's discuss several points about change that will give us a better background for later examining the process of change.

1. Change Is Upsetting.

One of life's more upsetting experiences is change; whether it be of a job or an address, of friends or church, or of a shopping area or travel route, change is stressful for everyone. This happens because most of us are creatures of habit and familiarity; we get into a pattern or a style of doing something and anything else is different and, therefore, produces anxiety. Even if the familiar way isn't the best for us, and at times even when it is harmful, we feel that we know what to expect; the familiar is better than the unknown.

Another reason why change is unsettling is that it usually sets off a chain reaction; one change often leads to several others. So it's not one upset—it's several upsets. Change does not occur in a vacuum; it generally necessitates other changes that are felt throughout the system.

The best way to deal with the upsetting aspect of change is to anticipate that things are going to be different for a while. You need to put on your seatbelt and open your eyes to the new scenery you will be seeing. As you see yourself reacting to change, you can try to sit on your own shoulder and ask yourself how this change feels. Usually, even if you make a positive change, it feels different, unsettling—maybe weird. It can give you the sensation that you don't know yourself. And, since change doesn't occur in a vacuum, you have to realize those around you will be different as well.

145

Because change is so upsetting, one must be strongly motivated to make change in one's life. This is often why people come to therapy when they absolutely cannot stand the way things are another minute. They feel as though they have been beating their heads against a wall and are ready to believe that "anything is better than this."

The motivation to change develops from two reasons: (1) the present approach to the situation isn't working; *and* (2) you are unhappy with yourself and the way you are acting. The first point is the easier one to see, but the second must be there in order for change to begin.

2. Change Means Self-Change.

When I mention the word "change" to participants at a workshop, their defenses usually go up. This seems strange at first because people generally come to a workshop on family matters to improve some aspect of their family life. But most people connect change with coercion and think that something is going to be forced upon them against their will. This early programming may be connected to the type of change we were all familiar with as kids, that is, when a parent said, "I would like you to change . . . (this or that behavior)." Since our parents were considerably bigger and more powerful, that statement had an undercurrent of coercion. Therefore, as adults, whenever someone mentions change we automatically dig in our heels and resist.

Change is something that most people say they want but are unwilling to work at because it is so difficult. Yet, most people enter counseling because they say they want change. Change is often defined incorrectly and, therefore, the process is misunderstood. Too often change is thought of as something we do to (or that happens to) somebody else because it is so much easier to project the need for change onto the other person. Of course, it couldn't be "wonderful me" that needs to change! Listen to the usual presentation of the problem by the changeseeker:

    a) "Joe has to be warmer and more affectionate to me."

    b) "He has to cut down on his drinking . . . it's getting serious."

    c) "She has to stop nagging me about everything and making me feel guilty all the time . . ."

    d) "I just can't go on like this . . . he's got to change."

146

e) "This women's movement has gotten her so assertive I can't stand her anymore."

f) "This kid is driving us crazy . . . he's got to get his act together."

It so often sounds as if somebody else has to do something— someone else has to go first in the change process, while the person wanting the change sits back hoping to observe and orchestrate the process.

The reality, however, is that the only change we can make is self-change; we cannot change others, only ourselves. This is a very hard lesson to learn because it would be so much easier if we didn't have to see the part we played in maintaining the problem. Blaming the other person completely and hoping that you can force him or her to change does not work. You have to take responsibility for yourself and the part you are playing in maintaining the dysfunction; this is the hardest step to take and change cannot occur until you know your part in the process.

Let's take the litany of complaints listed above by the change-seeker and restate them in a way that will make self-change more possible.

a) "What is it about me that makes it hard for Joe to be warmer and more affectionate to me?"

b) "How am I collaborating in this drinking problem? Am I feeling responsible for it?"

c) "I wonder if there is any validity to what she says—I do love her—so how come we are always in these nagging battles? What part of me is keeping them going?"

d) "If I were really serious, why haven't I done something?"

e) "What is it about me that doesn't like a woman that will speak her mind? I like those qualities in men. Is it the qualities I don't like or does something else get triggered in me?"

f) "I wonder what is making him act up so much . . . could it be anything that is going on within the family that has him upset?"

Once you work on yourself, figure out how you contribute to the problem, or how you might collaborate in it, the change process is under way.

Two things have convinced me about the difficulty of making changes in oneself. First, I've tried it myself and know how much easier it is to point out what is wrong with the other person in the dyad and ask him or her to change. It is human nature, I guess, to look for the easy way out; but that is just a temporary solution—like getting into a triangle when stress in the dyad gets too intense. No significant or lasting change takes place when we force someone else to change; we can only be in charge of ourselves and, therefore, can only change ourselves.

Secondly, if the change process was easier, few families would experience significant problems; individuals would have already changed those things about themselves that they know get them into relationship problems. Change can be a very painful process because it is recognizing that "wonderful me" is part of the problem and that there is an uphill fight to turn this process around, sometimes with little or no help in the beginning from the rest of the family.

3. Resistance to Change Is Natural.

Change is very difficult because there is a natural pull within the family to resist change and to maintain the status quo. Since the familiar is more comfortable than the new and the different, family members try to prevent the member seeking change from upsetting the system. The change-seeker often finds him/herself out there alone, with little or no support and encouragement from family; at this point many people often give up and fall back "into line."

Resistance to change within the family system is predictable. Since the family has already established a balance which makes most of the members more or less comfortable, family members will naturally resist change because it will be new, different and, for at least some period of time, anxiety producing. This does not mean that those family members who resist change are bad; they are just more familiar and more comfortable with the status quo and not sure that this new change will be any better.

This piece of information should be helpful in keeping individuals who are trying to change from getting too discouraged when their family tries to pull them back into line; they convey the message by their actions and words—"change back!" This is a normal process; don't let it throw you. The change that you are trying to make for yourself is most likely difficult for you; therefore, from your understanding of chain reactions, you can predict that it must be upsetting to those connected to you as well. Family members resist not because they are bad but because all change is upsetting. So, even when your changes look to be so clearly geared in a positive direction, don't be surprised to find some resistance—both obvious and subtle—to your efforts.

4. Change Must Be "Doable."

It is also extremely important that a change be "doable." This means one must pick a specific goal by which to measure progress. You can't say "I want to make a lot of money," without defining how much is "a lot." To one person it could be $30,000 a year, to another $100,000. The problem with a vague goal is that you never know if you've accomplished anything. "Doable" means that the change-seeker should always pick a goal that is manageable and not too big for the beginning. You can always continue the process once you see some success.

Human beings need to be able to measure progress and to have some way to define whether they have or have not achieved anything. In therapy, the client picks a particular problem, an issue, that represents the larger issue of achieving comfort in the situation. The larger issue may be that the couple has had trouble communicating about differences, and patterns have formed that are uncomfortable for both. Once the patterns have set in, communicating about them is that much more difficult. What must happen before communicating about patterns is that someone must make a move to change one of them. This may not automatically produce a relationship with more emotional sharing, but it has the benefit of giving one of the partners the peace of mind that he or she is taking action.

Sometimes people think that simply because behavior "B" clearly appears to be a better choice than does "A," change will

Figure 6-1

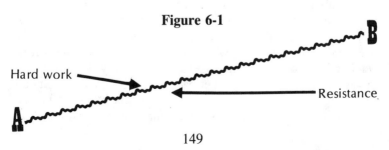

be easy and the other people involved will be able to change smoothly and immediately (*Figure 6-1*). However, there is always some resistance to change. Let's take a look at Joe and Kate (*Figure 6-2*) and see how this applies.

Figure 6-2

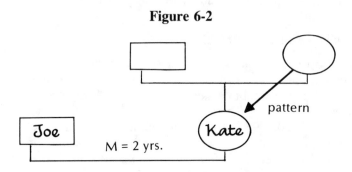

They have been married for two years, and a pattern has developed over the last year whereby Joe comes home late from work, having failed to call Kate to let her know that he's going to be delayed. She is furious with him when he arrives home, a fight ensues, and they have a lousy evening together. Kate decided to come in for counseling because she felt her marriage was falling apart.

I first asked Kate how come it seemed so important that she and Joe always have dinner together. She related that this was an important family tradition in her family; that her father worked as a laborer and that her mother always had a nice, hot meal ready for him when he came home. I also asked her how her father reacted to these efforts made by his wife because I was looking to see if there was any repetition of a pattern from Kate's family of origin. Well, it turns out that her father never really appreciated the work her mother went through to put a good meal on the table; it was taken for granted most of the time except on those rare nights when some emergency would prevent her mother from doing it and then her father would be furious with her. So it looked as though Kate was trying to carry on a pattern from her family of origin (family meals) which really doesn't appear to have worked too well for her parents. Like most of us, I guess she thought that she could make it work better by trying harder. Joe, on the other hand, comes from a family of eight where meals

150

were always scarce, taken on the run and seldom eaten as a group. The few occasions where the whole family came together for a meal usually turned out to be a family fight.

I asked Kate if she and Joe had talked about setting up a pattern around meals—like agreeing to eat together each night at a set time, etc. She said "no," they hadn't and, in fact, Joe usually didn't care that much about meals or whether he had to fix his own or eat it by himself when he got home late. I then asked Kate how long she had been waiting for Joe to change, that is, come home on time, call if he was going to be late, and maybe even appreciate her efforts at preparing a nice meal. Her response was, "A year and a half." I asked her if she waited a little longer and nagged him even more did she think that it might make a difference. She didn't think so and, besides, she was tired of nagging and said, "With the mood I am in when he gets home late, that is, disappointed and furious, I am not sure that I would want to come home to someone like me."

Kate is in a good place to make a change—the present way doesn't work and she is unhappy with her own behavior in the matter. I decided to coach Kate to take a new position—not a very drastic one, just a small change that she could make instead of waiting for Joe to change. Since she told me that she and Joe had agreed that 7:00 P.M. was a good time to plan on having dinner, I suggested that she review with Joe the plans for having dinner together one more time . . . with a little switch. She would plan dinner for 7:00 P.M. and if Joe wasn't home she would eat without him (which was not her first choice) and he could cook for himself.

She explained to Joe that she was doing this because she didn't want to be angry with him when he got home late and she had been holding the meal. Joe said he understood her feelings and that he would try to get home on time. The next night Kate had dinner ready at 7:00 P.M., but there was no sign of Joe. She waited until 7:30 and still there was no sign of Joe (she waited because change is hard and she hoped Joe would change first). So at 7:30 she ate her dinner and began to relax for the evening. Joe walked in at about 8:45 P.M. with his usual account of a difficult day at the office and how the trains had delayed him from getting home any earlier. When Joe found out that Kate had already eaten and he had to fend for himself, he was furious.

This is where Kate almost got pulled back into the old dysfunctional pattern; she had been clear with Joe about her new position, but she somehow thought that Joe would like it and go along smoothly with the change.

I said "almost got pulled back" because I had predicted with Kate before she tried this new position what the typical response might be from Joe. In this way she was not taken by surprise. She did not allow herself to get pulled into a big argument with Joe—just remained calm and expressed her regret about the train being late (which was a constant and legitimate problem). Kate was shocked, however, the next evening when Joe was not home at 7:00 P.M. She thought that if she could take a different position once then Joe would fall into line. No way. For several weeks Joe continued to arrive home late, sometimes fixing his own meals and sometimes eating at a fast-food restaurant. She generally ate by herself and began to fix fewer gourmet meals. There was still some tension between Kate and Joe about the change, but the time they now shared together in the evenings was much better than before. After about two months Joe asked if they could try having one meal during the week together because he kind of missed it. Kate agreed to try it and it has worked satisfactorily ever since. She is getting a little more of what she likes and the balance seems to be better for them; Kate needs to be cautious, however, about trying to extend it from one meal to five meals together the second week.

5. It Takes Only One Person to Begin the Change Process.

The person who knows that the present way isn't working can only begin by changing himself/herself. You need not, in fact should not, wait for someone else to initiate the change. It would be a lot easier if everyone figured out the part they played in the problem and began to change it; that seldom happens. It usually takes one person to take the initiative and be the catalyst for change and then maybe others will follow.

Change can take place within the family system as long as there is one person who is willing to stop the dysfunctional flow of the family, that is, stop playing his or her part in maintaining the problem. As soon as one person begins self-change instead of trying to change the other person, the deadlock in the system has been broken and there is now space and flexibility for others also to move, if they so choose. Be careful, however. One might say to oneself: "I know the part I play in this problem and I am going to change it." So you go about trying to do it differently. My caution is that just because you have decided to change yourself you might get very righteous about your good efforts and expect that everyone else in your family system should get on the bandwagon. Not so. People change at different times and at different paces. You must have minimal expectations about the other person's also changing. Otherwise you really haven't changed yourself; you are trying to manipulate the other, trying to change someone other than yourself.

Let's take an example where we can see some of these five points applied in the change process. Figure 6-3 depicts Jean and Phil Shaw, who have been married for ten years and have two children. Phil and his father are both alcoholics; Jean was and is an overresponsible oldest child in her family of origin.

Figure 6-3

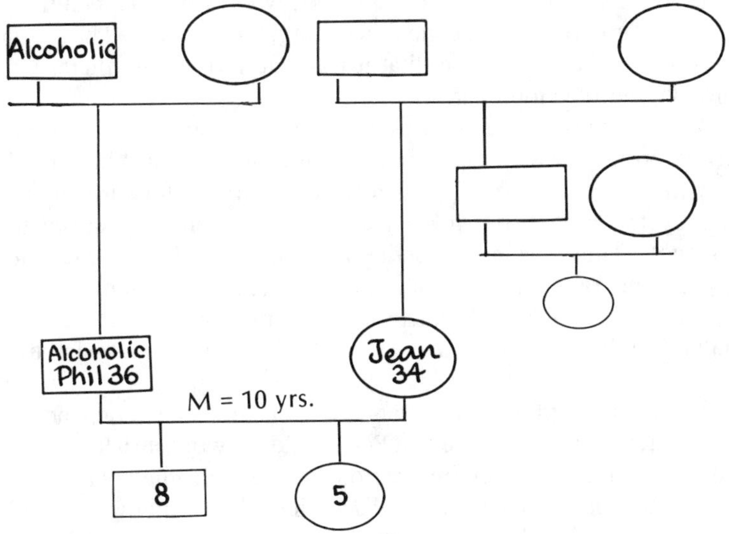

Jean has been trying to change Phil's drinking problem for a long time. She knew that Phil drank while they were dating but thought that after they were married she'd get him to change. Jean decided through therapy to take a new look at the part she played in contributing to his drinking. She has decided that she can't change Phil, only herself. Jean was able to see that she didn't mind Phil's drinking in the beginning because it enabled him to be more affectionate and better able to share his feelings. She realized that being overresponsible for his drinking was taking the responsibility away from Phil, where it belonged, and she decided to stop covering up for him when he couldn't go to work because of hangovers. Jean joined Al-Anon and began to tell the children to start bringing their friends home from school again—the cover-up was over. People would be welcome in their home again, the shades would be lifted, and they were not going to hide anymore. They had to go on with their lives and not be completely focused on their father's drinking. Jean and the kids had spent hours each day worrying about what would happen if Dad came home drunk, what would happen if they had any friends over to the house and anyone saw him, what would happen if he couldn't go to work the next morning, and so on. They had become so focused on him that it was interfering with their own growth and development.

The changes that Jean was making were bound to have an effect on the system. Jean was thinking that maybe Phil would stop drinking and join the family on its move forward in the life cycle. However, Phil began to drink more (resistance to change). This was not a deliberate move by Phil to escalate things, but rather is an example of how family systems work. When you are trying to make changes in a system, there is a natural pull from the other part of the system to resist the change.

So, as Jean moved to a more responsible and independent position, it was predictable that Phil would get worse in a last-ditch attempt to pull her back into her old overresponsible position. If Phil could get Jean to change back, he'd be changing her and then he would not have the hard work of self-change to undergo. Through counseling, Jean was able to maintain her own new position of getting her life and the kids' lives back on track. She did not separate from Phil but separated from the drinking focus.

Phil hit bottom, joined AA, and the family began its way back to being a more functional system.

Change begins with self. Change starts in the family system when one of its members decides to change the part he or she is playing in contributing to the problem. When times get tough and the rest of the system tries to pull that person back, that person must stick to the position that change is necessary and recognize that it is impossible to change anyone but oneself. The hope is that, while a person can only change self, in the process others may also learn how change works and reach a level of higher functioning and better balance.

The Three-Step Process of Change

Now that you have a better understanding of some of the components involved in change, let's take a look at the three-step process of change described by Carter and McGoldrick (1976). They say, "If you can change the part you play in your family's process, and hold it despite the family's reaction, while keeping in emotional contact with them, the family will change to accommodate your change." Therefore, a change requires at least three steps: (1) the change itself, (2) the family's reaction to the change, and (3) dealing with the family's reaction to the change. Most people do the two-step, that is, they change, but as soon as someone gets upset with them and says "change back" they do so. Let's use the Carter and McGoldrick approach in the case of Joe and Bev Vecchio and demonstrate how it works.

Figure 6-4 depicts the Vecchio family. The presenting complaint from Bev was that Joe was over-close to his widowed mother and that he was more a son to his mother than a husband to his wife. This had been the case for a long time and had been demonstrated particularly in the pattern of Joe's mother coming to dinner every Sunday. Bev stated that she wanted Joe's mother to come on fewer Sundays, but Joe was unwilling to agree to this.

Joe admitted that he was quite close to his mother and, as her only child, felt a strong obligation to take care of her. This relationship between Joe and his mother had intensified over the years due to the stressful and distant relationship between his father and mother, and the death of Joe's father ten years ago had caused the fusion to become even more evident. Joe said he

Figure 6-4

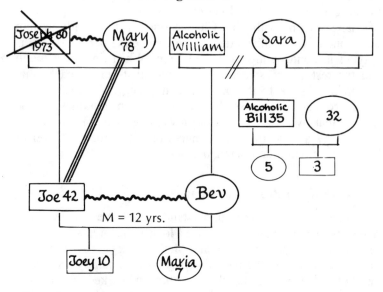

couldn't understand what Bev had against "this nice, little old lady"—his mother wasn't going to live forever, so why couldn't Bev put up with it a little longer?

Bev and Joe attended a workshop* that I had given to their PTA group on "Understanding Family Patterns and the Change Process," and shortly thereafter Bev and Joe contacted me to discuss this problem. Both Joe and Bev came to the first session and gave me a general overview of what had been happening. Joe refused to come back, stating that he didn't believe in this "counseling stuff" and that he only came this once to please his wife. Joe's presence wasn't really needed at this point in therapy because he wasn't interested in changing—he was not that unhappy with the situation, it was Bev who was unhappy and she would have to take the initiative to start the change process. Let me point out that it would have been nice if Joe wanted to change because he knew that he was part of the problem and that he had an unhappy wife, but he didn't. He was going to resist change and hope that Bev wasn't really serious; perhaps if he didn't

*This refers to a 4-session, 8-hour preventive educational workshop that teaches family operating principles in order to reduce stress and improve family functioning.

come with her for counseling she might also stop. Bev remembered from the workshop that change meant self-change and that you can't wait for the other person in the relationship to change first when you're the unhappy one. She decided to come for counseling alone and to work on her part of the problem. She was really disappointed that Joe wouldn't come too, but that didn't stop her. Although Bev had remembered most of the principles about change from the workshop, it was interesting to see how strong the pull is for each of us to try to get the other person to change. It is a very common practice for one member of a couple to bring the other to a therapist in hope that the therapist will change him or her and accomplish what the other spouse has been trying in vain to do for years. That never works!

Let's now take a look at some of the dialogue between Bev and me in order to understand some of the background that led to the development of the problem.

Therapist: Bev, if you were able to change your part in the struggle with Joe regarding his mother, what changes would that make in your life?"

Bev: I'm not sure. We have fought over this situation for so long that it has made it very difficult for us to be close and affectionate toward each other. As you said in the workshop, things sometimes get worse before they get better when you start counseling because you have to look at the real problem instead of the symptoms.

Therapist: Are you saying that Joe's mother is just the symptom of some problem between you and Joe?

Bev: I think so. Remember the triangles that you drew in the workshop? Well, the example of the triangle with the couple and the mother-in-law really hit home to me. I had been saying all along that the only problem between Joe and me was his mother; now I think it is more than that.

Therapist: How did the separation process work in *your* family?"

Bev: I think that Joe and I never got close . . .

Therapist: Bev, since Joe is not here, let's just try to see *your* part in the development of closeness in your marriage.

Bev: Well . . . it's a lot easier to talk about Joe's part in it.

Therapist: I know, but he's not here right now.

157

Figure 6-5

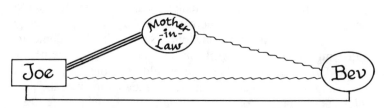

Bev: Well, I came from an Irish family where no one ever shared their real feelings and closeness was never openly expressed. I think that you were supposed to know that you were loved because there was food on the table and because you just knew that parents were supposed to love their children. My father was an alcoholic and my mother nagged him all the time; the nagging was so bad that I didn't blame him, after a while, for drinking and not coming home. I kind of decided to be just the opposite from my mother; I was going to find myself a good man with a caring family (who wouldn't drink), be supportive of him and definitely not nag him all the time.

Therapist: Has it worked?

Bev: Well, I found a good man from a caring family. The problem is that they care so much about each other that Joe puts his family, especially his mother, before me. I was, however, very supportive of Joe and tried very hard to be a good wife and not nag him. I thought peace and harmony were worth the price of keeping my mouth shut when things made me unhappy. I think that this is my big part in this dilemma. After keeping my mouth shut for the first ten years of our marriage and being the good, dutiful wife, I began to realize that I wasn't happy and, generally speaking, I've been nagging him quite a bit for the last two years. What makes it worse is that I hate myself for being that way because I know what it did to my parents' relationship. I have allowed this pattern to develop and now that I want to change it I can understand that Joe is not going to like it. It would have been a lot easier if I had taken a position regarding his mother, which really was our lack of closeness, twelve years ago.

Therapist: If Joe's mother is the symptom, then are you saying that closeness is the issue between you and Joe?

Bev: I think so. That's pretty scary.

158

Therapist: How come?

Bev: What happens if I am successful at getting my mother-in-law out of the picture and then find out that there isn't enough closeness between Joe and me to hold the marriage together?

Therapist: This change process is risky because there are no guarantees about what the end result will be. Maybe we should stop now?

Bev: No, I am not expecting any guarantees. . . . I can't go on living like this. . . . I am unhappy with myself. . . . I feel used . . . but I have allowed it. I have to do something to change it.

Therapist: O.K., Bev, let's see what you can do. Let's just take a look at what closeness meant to *you* when you married Joe.

Bev: I was so happy to be able to get away from my parents—with all the fighting and drinking—Joe looked great to me. When I look back on it, I sometimes think that closeness might have meant just being away from them. See, Joe was a good man; he didn't drink, he didn't argue a lot, and his family got along well. I may have married him to get into a loving family.

Therapist: Did Joe's family let you in?

Bev: That's interesting. In the beginning they didn't. . . . I couldn't cook pasta or hang out in the kitchen with all the women at parties . . . but I worked so hard at it. I was deterined to be accepted by them. It probably wasn't until Joey was born that I finally began to feel accepted. I realize now what a big part I played in setting this mess up. They will all turn on me now.

Therapist: Do you have an understanding about how come you needed to be accepted by them so much and how come you allowed so much to happen before taking a better position for yourself?

Bev: I had no idea until you spoke about "cutoffs." I, in fact, had cut off my own family from the time I got engaged to Joe. Things got so bad that they didn't even come to the wedding. I have little or no contact with them now—but a part of me has always been missing them.

Therapist: Where are they now?

Bev: My parents got divorced a few years after I got married; my father lives alone and the last I heard was still drinking; my mother remarried, which I've never really gotten over; and my brother Bill has also turned out to be an alcoholic.

Therapist: What do you think cutting your own family off has to do with you and Joe?

Bev: You got me thinking after the workshop had ended that if I had cut off all of my own emotional connections to my own family of origin I was going to be going into my new marriage desperate to be accepted . . . therefore, willing to do almost anything. And that's what I did . . . kept my mouth shut and became a doormat. I was probably so starved for attention that I pursued Joe all over the place—and he really didn't like it. I couldn't understand what was happening.

Therapist: Well, let's begin with your taking a new position and see how that works. At a later date, if you have any interest, I might have some ideas about how you could have a little different relationship with your own family. But let's see how this thing with Joe goes first.

Bev: That's fine . . . but I think sometime I would like to do something with my own family.

I began coaching Bev on how to change her piece in the problem. I knew that we had to pick a goal for our work together that was specific and "doable." By "specific" I meant that Bev would have to define a goal that was measurable and clear and not pick something too general, such as—"I would like to feel better about Joe when this is over."

I asked Bev to define a goal for our work together. She thought that if she could *succeed* at having her mother-in-law come every other Sunday it would be a step in the right direction. Bev felt that this would not be too drastic a change; she did not want to eliminate altogether the visits by her mother-in-law. She thought that she probably could get to like the "old lady" if she didn't feel in second place to her and had some say in how the visiting was set up.

This was a pretty good beginning for Bev. However, Bev was still trying to get Mrs. Vecchio to change (that is, stop visiting so much) instead of doing the changing herself. So, after further consultation, Bev decided to tell Joe that she would be willing to see his mother every other Sunday if Joe still wanted to invite her, but that she would not necessarily be at home if Joe decided to invite his mother more often. In doing this, she was not asking Joe or his mother to change; rather, only Bev was making a

160

change. Bev realized that parents and children should have one-to-one relationships with each other without having to have their spouses present all the time. Problems usually occur when one spouse has trouble communicating with his/her parent and has to involve the other spouse all the time to help make conversation or take care of one's own parent (triangle). This was exactly what was happening with Joe and Bev; Joe really didn't know how to talk with his mother, so he would leave her with Bev in the kitchen and head for the television set and the afternoon ballgames where there was no danger of any communication taking place.

The Change Itself—Step 1. As we've learned, Bev decided that her new position would be to limit her visiting with, and availability to, Joe's mother to every other Sunday. Bev also knew that this was just a symptom (the tip of the iceberg) of the problem that she and Joe were having in establishing closeness in their relationship. She knew that she could no longer wait for Joe to one day decide not to invite his mother. She had become part of the problem as a result of being so accepting of what Joe wanted (out of balance) in an attempt to gain membership and acceptance into Joe's family. It was also clear to Bev that if she was successful in dealing with the symptom—getting Joe's mother to stay away for a while—she would then have to deal with the space and time that would be created by her absence. If Joe's mother weren't around every Sunday, would Joe and Bev be any closer, would they spend that time on Sunday in a more productive fashion that would generate more closeness and understanding? These are the real questions that have to be answered and the real goals behind her changing. Bev feels that the present family balance does not work for her; she is going to try to reestablish a new balance that will work better for her. Bev has been alerted to the fact that there are no guarantees that the new balance she is trying to establish will be any better and has been coached to be prepared for the reality that probably no one else in the family will like the new structure because it will upset the familiar balance.

The Change Itself
"I will limit my visiting with and
availability to Joe's mother to
every other Sunday."

The Family's Reaction to the Change—Step 2. Joe was furious and reacted for the first two days by saying that this was not fair and who was Bev to change things that had been going on for years. Bev told Joe about her new limits on availability and that she would like to spend the following Sunday as a family—maybe she, Joe and the children could do something together. Joe was so upset that he didn't hear or care about what her new plans were. After being furious in the beginning of the week, and seeing that Bev was not backing down and that she was still firm in her position, Joe decided to stop talking to her. This, in the past, had always made Bev very upset and had generally made her give in to what Joe wanted. This time was different. Before Bev took this new position we had gone over in advance all the possible reactions that Joe might have to her new position. We both knew that he wasn't going to like it so it only made sense to be ready for his unhappy response. Bev predicted that he would be furious for a few days and then he would probably stop talking to her. Knowing this in advance helped Bev to keep her perspective and her resolve.

It was not Joe's reaction that almost upset her resolve, but two other events that occurred mid-week. First, Joe's mother called on Wednesday to ask how Bev was doing and was she feeling all right. Bev almost went through the ceiling because Joe's mother never called and seldom asked Bev how she was feeling. Bev immediately thought that Joe had called his mother and that the two of them were in a coalition against her. She was about to blast her mother-in-law when she got hold of herself and realized how emotionally reactive situations such as this one can be.

This phone call was a nice gesture made, in Bev's eyes, for the wrong reasons. But whether the mother-in-law had been called by Joe or not (and it turned out that Joe had not, at this point, told his mother anything, hoping that he could get Bev to fall back into line), Bev had been coached not to allow herself to be thrown by the reactions of other family members who she knew weren't going to like the change she was planning. The mother-in-law's phone call could be understood as an interesting coincidence or as the intricate and mysterious workings of a family system; that is, when change is about to take place in a family system, sometimes there are unknowing signs or vibrations given

162

off that make people aware that something is about to happen. They often respond unknowingly in an attempt to maintain the status quo.

The second event that almost threw Bev was the reaction of her children. On Friday morning before Joey and Maria went off to school Joey asked: "Mom, are you and Dad going to get a divorce?" Bev was stunned and, as she sat there speechless, she listened to both Joey and Maria pour out their concerns.

Maria asked first, practically in tears: "How come you and Dad are always fighting about Grandma? Don't you like her? Don't you feel sorry that she lives alone?" Joey followed with his worries. "Mom, please don't get divorced and please stop fighting with Dad. I don't like Grandma coming every Sunday either, but at least it keeps Dad happy. See what happens when you start this stuff about not letting Grandma come this Sunday. [He has noticed how Bev's position has been changed.] Dad's been furious ever since you said that . . . everybody is tense and nervous. He is mad at us kids, too."

Bev tried to assure them that it was not that serious, and she tried to calm their fears as she rushed them off to make the bus. She told them that she would talk with them when they came home from school that day and answer all their questions. As Bev closed the door behind the kids, she sat down and wondered: is this all worth it?

Bev had a counseling appointment that morning and she was feeling pretty discouraged as she prepared to leave for the meeting. Just as she was about to leave, the phone rang. It was Joe—calling to ask her if she had called to invite his mother for Sunday. Bev was about to give in—it seemed so much easier than holding her new position—but said, "I'll talk to you later this afternoon."

When Bev reached my office, she felt overwhelmed. She knew that it wasn't going to be easy, but she had no idea that everyone would be against her. I explained to her that she was at the crossroads of the change process. Most people get this far; this is the easy part. It is easy to moan and groan about something that we feel is unfair or out of balance, but it is a completely different story to go through the pain and suffering required to turn it around.

It is at this exact crossroad that most people seeking change fall short. As soon as someone says, "Change back!" they do it.

Once this happens, change is so much harder the next time. Who is going to believe you or take you seriously? They will say, "You are just a lot of talk . . . you do not mean it."

It was very important at this point to make sure that Bev wanted to continue the change process; it is crucial that she want the change for herself and not for the therapist, because she is the one who will have to live with the results. I said to Bev: "Maybe your situation isn't that bad . . . you have been able to put up with this situation for almost twelve years . . . maybe you can tolerate it a little longer."

Bev responded: "It's worse than ever. I can't stand it anymore. If I give in now, I'll hate myself even more. My husband, my kids—they all want me to lie back down and be a doormat so that Dad doesn't get upset. What about me! Doesn't anybody care how I am feeling? I am going to call Joe and tell him that I never want his mother to set foot in my house again."

The Family's Reaction to the Change
They say, "CHANGE BACK!"

Dealing with the Family's Reaction to the Change—Step 3.

Bev was pretty upset at this point, but it is important for her not to let her emotional upset overwhelm her when thinking about the position that she wants to maintain. To fly off the handle at this point would not have been helpful for her goal. Everything that had happened so far is quite understandable to someone who knows how a family system operates; that is, the family members are going to resist change which appears to be for the better, not because they are bad people but because there is a natural resistance to anything which is being introduced into the family system that is new and different. Even when the family subtly knows that the present way is not that productive, there is still a resistance by the family members to change it. Bev was alerted to this earlier on in the counseling sessions but, even after she was warned to be on the alert for this strong tendency in families to maintain the status quo, it was hard to remember when her anxiety was so high. This is the part that stops many people from moving on to the third step in the change process, which is dealing with the family's reaction to your change.

My first job was to get Bev back into a thinking position rather than an emotional position on these latest developments. After a few "You told me so's but I didn't think it would happen that way in my family," Bev was able to see that they were not bad people but just trying to take the easier way out for themselves. As she began to get her emotions under control, we began to look at the position she would like to take with Joe and the children. It was the reaction of the children that seemed to throw her the most; she expected Joe not to like the new arrangements, but she never expected the children to try to get her to give in.

We began with Joe and how best to deal with him. Bev decided, after some coaching, to speak with Joe at home that evening. She clearly stated that she was not going to invite his mother for Sunday because she was planning a family picnic for just the four of them. She told Joe that she hoped that he would come but that she knew it would be hard for him not to be with his mother as usual on Sunday. If he chose not to come, she'd be unhappy but she would have to deal with that. She told him that she knew how important it was for a mother and son to have a good relationship and that she was not trying to ruin that but that she needed to have more time with Joe, both alone and with the children. Basically, there was a need for better balance in these relationships. Joe's response was angry, and he stormed out of the room leaving Bev with no idea about what he was going to do.

With the little energy that Bev had left, she gathered Joey and Maria together to discuss what was happening. She explained to them that the arguing between her and their father was adult business, it did not involve them, and they should stay out of it. She knew that it was upsetting to them but that it was all right for parents to quarrel. They would work it out. She explained to them that she had made a big mistake many years ago in trying to please everyone except herself. (This was not easy to admit to her children, but it was the truth and was better than blaming the children's father or grandmother for doing something to her.) This tendency had gotten her to feel badly about herself and she was now trying to change that. She explained that she did not like having Grandma over for dinner every Sunday because she felt used and stuck in the kitchen all day and had no time with Joe or them. She knew that her change was going to upset them but that she hoped that they would try to understand it. Bev also spoke with Joey and Maria about how patterns get repeated from one generation to the next, and that her pattern of trying to please everyone else before herself was not a good practice to teach them. She tried to show the children what part she had played in this mother-in-law situation while at the same time trying to teach them a lesson of not blaming somebody else for her situation.

Sunday finally came and Joe's mother did not come. Joe refused to tell Bev what he had told his mother regarding the fact that she was not invited (which one could have predicted in advance), and he did not accompany Bev and the children on the family picnic. It was rather a tense day, to say the least, but one could not have expected it to go smoothly the first time.

The following week Joe, as usual, asked Bev to invite his mother for Sunday dinner. Bev said that she was available to have his mother for dinner but that Joe would have to call to invite her since it was his mother. Joe began to bristle at this a little bit but decided not to make an issue out of it, figuring his mother was coming—thank God—let's leave it at that. I had suggested this change to Bev because part of Bev's role in this triangle was to be the "switchboard operator" in the communication pattern between Joe and his mother.

Bev was, in fact, feeling much different about her mother-in-law. She went a little out of the way to serve something special. She felt that she had some control over the visit because it wasn't a command performance ordered by her husband. The visit went well; nothing was said about the previous Sunday and everyone for the first time in a long time seemed to have a good time.

Early that next week I had another session scheduled with Bev. She reported how well things had turned out and that her goal was almost accomplished. I congratulated her on the hard work that she had accomplished, but cautioned her about how her family would continue to resist the change by trying to revert to the still-familiar pattern. I predicted that it might be a little too early to tell whether or not Joe had really accepted the new Sunday routine—that the coming weekend would give a better indication if the four of them could do something together as a family or if she and Joe could spend some time alone. After all, the frequency of the mother-in-law's visits was only a symptom; the real test would come after the change, when Bev and Joe would see if they could establish a better sense of closeness than they had previously.

Bev left that session thinking that I was overly cautious but prepared for the system to try to regain its old form. Thursday night at dinner Joe asked Bev if she had called his mother yet to invite her to dinner on Sunday. Bev couldn't believe her ears! She thought to herself: "Doesn't this guy ever give up?" At that point Joey, who had admitted the previous week that he really didn't like Grandma coming every Sunday either but that it at least kept Dad happy and off everyone's back, chimed in with, "Yeah, we had a pretty good time last Sunday." Here was another chance for Bev to throw in the towel—allow herself to be trampled upon. She kept her calm, reached for her glass of water, and said: "Joe, I know that you care about your mother, but I need time with you, too. I was hoping that you and I could go do something together without the kids or your mother."

"Are you still on this kick? I'll bet the therapist is telling you to do this."

"That's not true, Joe. He may have some ideas about how I can be a little happier and more fulfilled, but I'm the one who has decided to do the changing. I really enjoyed having your mother here last week and I might just get to like having her a little more if you didn't cram her down my throat every week."

"What am I going to tell my mother if she can't come again this week?"

"I don't know what you should say to her—that's between you and her. I am going to have enough problems trying to deal with my own parents without trying to deal with your mother, too. Maybe you could go to talk to the therapist. I've found the counseling very useful."

"What would I talk to him about?"

"That's up to you, Joe." She then continued eating.

Joe did come to see me by himself for a few sessions, not so much because he owned up to his part in the problem but because he began to realize that Bev was serious and not going to fall back into line. I worked with Joe and helped him realize that what he could do would be to develop a one-to-one relationship with his mother that did not involve talking about his wife or his children. This would not be easy for Joe since he had been letting Bev be the go-between for years. I encouraged him to spend time alone with his mother; he could go visit her at her apartment or telephone her during the week. Notice that I began this paragraph with "what he *could* do." However, Joe made minimal attempts to establish a better relationship with his mother. Joe took a few of the ideas that I offered to him but the situation between him and his mother didn't really change. Joe is not a bad person for not working harder on his relationship with his mother; it just is not a top priority for him.

Joe and Bev are doing better; their situation is not completely resolved but there is more balance in the relationship. They are learning to spend time together, which is not easy for any couple to do. They are trying hard not to let something else, like a child or hobby, distract them from working on the closeness that was missing in their relationship.

In concluding this vignette about change, a few points become clear: change is not easy, there is always resistance to it, and it only takes one person to begin the change process. Let's now apply what we have learned about the change process to two important questions left unanswered from earlier chapters: "How can I change my distancing/pursuing style of emotional interaction?" (Chapter 7) and "How can I get out of a triangle (change) once I realize that I am in one?" (Chapter 8).

CHAPTER SEVEN

Changing Your Style
of Emotional Interaction

WHEN YOU read the different tendencies of distancers and pursuers in Chapter 2, were you thinking "that sounds like my spouse," "my father really fits that distancer description," or "my sister must have been a pursuer?" If you were, you are probably like most people who hear this concept for the first time; that is, they try to see how the significant people in their lives fit into it and they tend not to look for themselves in the descriptions. However, the first step in making a change in your relationship style is to review the "P and D" chart in Chapter 2, looking to see which style of emotional interaction you tend to have. After you have an idea of how you generally operate, ask yourself if you're happy with it or if you would like to change it. If you are satisfied and do not desire any change at this time, that's fine. If your style is working for you, cultivate it and enjoy it. But, if you have decided that you would like to change some aspect of *your* style of emotional interaction, read on.

Pursuers, generally speaking, are more interested in changing the relationship, are willing to take a few more emotional risks, are more hopeful that relationships can improve, and are usually more active in such pursuits. However, pursuers often make the mistake of defining change in the relationship as changing the distancer to be less distant. By now you are well aware that this type of change doesn't work; the only real change is when we change ourselves. Sometimes pursuers can also get themselves into difficulties by viewing their tendencies—such as wanting more closeness and wanting it now rather than later—as being better than those of the distancer. This righteous stance sometimes keeps them from seeing their part in the relationship balance. It takes two to have an imbalance in a relationship: that is, one doing too much and the other not doing enough, and both pursuing and distancing contribute equally to the problem. Distancers also desire change in relationships but usually they are slower to become aware of the relationship problem and do not seek change to the same degree as a pursuer might. Let's begin with the pursuer who seeks change in his or her relationship style.

For Pursuers

Pursuers should first of all follow Tom Fogarty's rule—"Never pursue a distancer" (Fogarty, 1979).

Figure 7-1

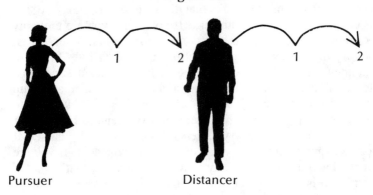

Pursuer   Distancer

When you pursue a distancer, you guarantee that he or she will move further away, thus initiating what Murray Bowen calls the "two-step" (*Figure 7-1*). Initial pursuit might move the distancer two steps away; repeated pursuit might result in distances of even greater proportions (*Figure 7-2*) as the distancer tries harder to get "leave me alone" across to the pursuer.

If you are a pursuer, you will have some firsthand understanding of how this works. When the person you are pursuing tells you, in any number of ways, to back off, you will have pet responses, such as: "All I was trying to do was help," "I only kept asking you because I wanted you to know I cared," or "Why do you always clam up when I'm around?" As a pursuer you generally mean well: that is, you are thinking about the other person but you are also trying to have a need of yours met—more closeness. That's where the hitch comes in—in that even when you realize that your pursuit is having the opposite effect from what you desired, you still tend to want to pursue.

Figure 7-2

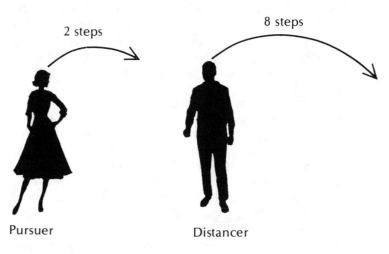

2 steps   8 steps

Pursuer   Distancer

The reasons for this are: first, pursuing is your most comfortable style of relating to others; and, secondly, you are much more comfortable being involved and preoccupied with someone else's feelings, upsets and emotions than with your own. Since you really care about the distancer, try to view objectively your situation and say, "Pursuing my spouse or my child just isn't working; I'm willing to consider and then maybe try another approach." That new approach has to be to give him or her additional space. Doing this will not be easy, or your preference, because this is not your distinctive style; but it will give the distancer what he or she has been seeking—a little more space. Caring for the other means trying to balance your needs and his or her needs. Distancers like their space, so give them some. Once pursuers can accept that pursuing a distancer does not work and realize that as long as they continue the pursuit the distancer will stay at least two steps away from them, then the stage is set for the first major shift in the relationship system to occur.

How to Back Off. Pursuers must first back off! At this point pursuers sometimes say, "Why must I change first . . . why can't the distancer just move toward me or stop moving away?" The answer to that goes back to our definition of what "change" is.

"Change" is self-change; it is something that one does to oneself for oneself. One makes change when the present way of operating is not working and when one is unhappy with the part his or her behavior plays in the problem. So, before a pursuer can have any hope of successfully pulling back, he or she would have to be convinced that pursuing is not the answer and be willing to do some hard work.

Why is change such hard work? Generally, people find it difficult to admit that "wonderful me" might be part of the problem. I say "part of the problem" because in a relationship difficulties lie between the couple, rather than in one or the other person, and each person collaborates in maintaining the conflict. Unfortunately, it is easier to define the part the other person plays in the problem, point out to the other person what's wrong with him or her and how he or she should change, rather than to focus on whom we can control, namely, ourselves. The pursuer is usually moving at about 90 miles an hour in making suggestions about how the other person should change and this is why it is so hard to put on the brakes, back off, and put the focus on self. It always seems easier to try to coerce someone else into changing first. The hard work, however, is changing yourself, which most pursuers learn after many years and much frustration.

Pursuers Pulling Back. To stop pursuing, the pursuer must pull back from being overinvolved in the emotional space of the other person (usually a distancer). One would have to stop trying to find out what is going on in the other persons's gut, how he or she is feeling, what makes him or her tick, and what wonderful thoughts are going on in his or her head that are not being shared. This type of pursuit is experienced as an invasion and pushes the distancer further away (*Figure 7-3*).

Pursuers often feel that they are the emotional lifeline that keeps the distancer going and that if they were to back off, even just a little, the other person would instantly go downhill. (Examples of this are clearly seen in pursuing mothers who are overly involved with their children and in pursuing spouses who are overinvolved with their drinking and distant mates.)

At this point the pursuer seldom realizes that the pursuit and overinvolvement may be part of the problem. Pursuers feel that if they were to stop asking all the questions and taking all the initiative in the relationship there would be no communication

Figure 7-3

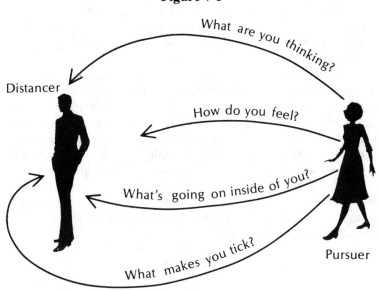

or relationship at all. They are afraid to pull back and find out whether or not there is any life left in the relationship. The very real fear is that if you pull back the other person will not communicate with you.

Pursuers must stop pursuing the feelings and emotional insides of the other person and take a look at what is going on inside themselves. While chasing after the emotions of the other person, the pursuer avoids looking at what is going on inside himself or herself. Pursuers tend not to talk about their own feelings; they would rather have others tell them about their feelings. For example, if you reversed the tables on a pursuer, this is how the conversation might go:

Pursuer: You are looking a little down today—how are you feeling?

Distancer: It's nothing. [Reverse:] By the way, how are you feeling?

Pursuer: I asked you first—come now, tell me what's happening with you.

173

The odd thing about this is that pursuers think they share a lot about how they are feeling but, in fact, most of them are so wrapped up in trying to get into the emotional space of another person that they seldom have a good sense of what is going on inside themselves.

What happens to the pursuer who changes his or her focus? The pursuer comes in touch with some of his or her own feelings of incompleteness, insecurity and loneliness. These are normal fears that we all have and which the pursuer has tried to avoid by working overtime on someone else's feelings. In an attempt not to deal with self, the pursuer generally becomes over-involved with one person, thus overloading that relationship. Figure 7-4 shows the pursuit and overinvolvement of the wife with her husband. The arrows represent excessive pursuit of the wife and the squiggly lines (〰〰〰〰) represent a troubled and distant connection with her parents.

Figure 7-4

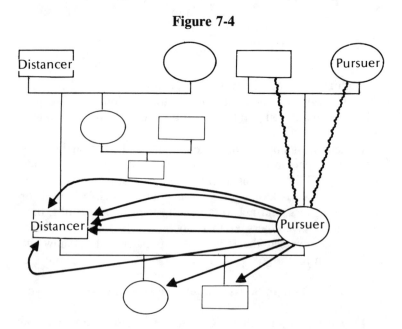

It also shows, perhaps, some of the reasons for the pursuit. If the wife, as an only child, is poorly connected to her family of origin, one might suspect that part of the reason for the overload in the marital dyad has to do with the wife's expectation that her husband would make up for what was missing in her relationship system with her parents. It is clear from the diagram that the marital relationship is overloaded and it will be just a matter of time before some symptom of stress surfaces.

An overloaded emotional relationship is very similar to an electrical circuit. When there is an electrical overload, something breaks down or blows up. A similar explosion often seen in emotional systems occurs when the distancer overreacts in an angry way to constant pursuit by driving the pursuer back or away through a heated argument. The pursuer has overloaded and burdened the relationship. Too much closeness or over-involvement often gives the other person a feeling of suffocation, which usually leads to an event (e.g., argument, separation) that will produce space and distance.

The Change Process. Having pulled back, the pursuer must now take a self-focus, which means being in touch with his or her own emotions and issues. This is hard work, but that's what self-change is all about. Let's explore how the change is likely to affect the pursuer and, secondly, to see what, if any, effect it has on the other person in the dyad, namely, the distancer.

(1) *The Change Itself.* This would involve pulling back, focusing on one's own feelings rather than on the other's emotions, and allowing the other person to have more emotional space.

If your natural inclination is to solve a problem now—wait. If you want to talk it over—think it over. If you need to make up immediately after a fight—try giving it some time. If you feel anxious about something and want comfort—try pampering yourself. If you're worried about where the relationship is going — worry about where you're going. If you're concerned about why your partner is reacting in such and such a way—try to figure out why you are reacting the way you are.

It is not that the talents of the pursuer are not vital to the relationship, but they may need to be redirected. It is a wonderful quality to care enough about the ones you love to want to work at it. You just need to take some of that valuable energy and give it back to "wonderful you."

Most pursuers are able to understand at this point that they have been working much too hard on trying to make the relationship

175

function. Some will admit to feeling exhausted and frustrated by their attempts. This results from putting too great a proportion of their emotional energies into one relationship. They are overloading that relationship and it is bound to wear them out and not benefit the relationship. Important questions to ask at this point are: How did this pursuing style of interaction develop and where did it come from? Was one born with this style or was it something learned growing up in one's family of origin? In asking these types of questions the pursuer is taking a self-focus. He/she is not blaming the other person for being distant or for not meeting his/her emotional needs, but is looking at himself or herself and trying to decide how this style developed.

Up to this point, the pursuer has been pulling back and staying out of the emotional space of the other person and has been trying to take a self-focus. (What am I feeling? What does that event set off inside of me?) He or she now needs to look back into his or her family of origin to understand where this pursuing style originated. As a pursuer you can do this by looking at your family genogram or a photo album and begin to reflect upon the different styles of interaction in the family. Flipping through the album you may remember distancing and pursuing tendencies in your parents and siblings; you may even be able to trace these tendencies back to your grandparents. You begin to see, as you pursue the family album and your genogram that your own style of interacting and relating didn't just happen but that it seems to be connected to what happened before you.

Figure 7-5 shows what a wife might discover when tracing her style of interaction back into her family of origin. A wife realizes that she has a pursuing style of interaction with her husband which often seems to be a problem between them. She begins to look back up her family tree and comes to the realization that her mother was, and still is, a pursuer in her relationship with her father. This woman can now afford to be more objective in viewing her parents' relationship than her own and she sees that her mother's pursuit of her father throughout their marriage had done nothing but cause arguments between them. Now the wife begins to realize that her tendency to pursue is very much like her mother's.

(2) *The System's Reaction to the Change.* It is at this step in the process that the individual who is seeking self-change runs

Figure 7-5

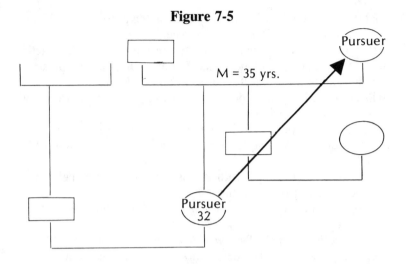

into his or her own resistance. The resistance usually takes this form: after trying to pull back for a short time (e.g., two weeks) and focusing on oneself, it often seems easier to go back to pursuing someone else's feelings rather than trying to understand your own. This occurs because the process is difficult and when the going gets tough people have a tendency to look for a familiar and easier way out. The best reason to forge ahead with the new approach is that one knows that his or her pursuing style has not worked.

As the pursuer, you have begun to pull back and to take a look inside yourself. You have become more self-focused than other-focused. You have begun to trace the origins of your emotional tendencies of relating back into your family of origin and you have started to rely more on yourself for your emotional needs rather than on the other person. You have been doing a lot of work, and hard work, too. It is very natural for you to wonder how your changing might be affecting your distancer. In your view of things, it would seem perfectly logical to hope for the other person to start moving closer to you. You *think* this way because you are a pursuer, but distancers are not likely to *act* that way. Systems theory teaches that if one person in a system (the pursuer) moves or changes, it is likely that someone else (the distancer) might also move. There is, however, no guarantee

177

that the movement will be in the direction the pursuer would like, or that it will take place on the pursuer's timetable.

I would caution the pursuer not to use pulling back as a tactic to get the distancer to come closer. For example, the manipulative pursuer might hope that if he or she pulls back then the distancer will come rushing in. It doesn't work that way. The reasons for pursuers to pull back are:

(a) they are convinced that pursuit doesn't work;

(b) they see their style as playing a part in the relationship problem; and

(c) they are unhappy with themselves for always being the pursuer, the nag or the initiator.

Hopes that the distancer will change because you, the pursuer, are changing may well backfire.

(3) *Dealing with the System's Reaction to the Change*. At this step the pursuer who has been working on self-change may ask, "What am I supposed to do with all this space, emptiness and energy I now have as a result of pulling back (changing) and giving the other person in the relationship some space?" Let's talk about dealing with this new situation.

We know that change in one person sets off a chain reaction in the system. Thus, when one person changes self, it is logical to think that it will be felt by or have some effect on others in the system, especially those to whom we are most connected. Let's consider some of the reactions that could occur when a pursuer stops pursuing.

(a) No change may occur.

This is always a possibility and occurs for two reasons. The first is that the pursuer has not pulled back far enough. Let's take two examples. If a pursuing parent has been overinvolved with a teenage youngster and routinely plays "20 Questions" with the youngster when he or she comes home from school by asking, "How did your day go?" "How are you feeling?" etc., then asking only 15 questions is progress, but probably not enough so that a real difference is felt by the teenager. In a marital relationship, if the pursuing spouse has to ask as soon as he or she gets home how the other person's day went, then waiting five minutes would be a small start, waiting thirty minutes would be much better and not asking at all (but waiting for the other person to initiate a discussion about how the day went) would be real progress. If you, as pursuer, are saying to yourself, "He or she would never ask me first," then you haven't waited long enough and haven't pulled back far enough.

The second reason that there may be no change is because the pursuer has not maintained his or her new position long enough. If you have been a constant pursuer, your distancer might think that you are just tired and worn out—that you are just catching your breath for the next push. Please remember that it takes time for change to be experienced. The pursuer wants things to happen quickly, if not immediately, and the distancer believes that change is a very gradual process.

I believe that if you have pulled back far enough and if you have maintained your self-focus for a long enough period of time (and this would depend on your particular situation), something will change in the relationship. There is no guarantee that the change will be your first choice, but some movement will occur.

(b) Some change occurs in the other person.

Let's consider two possibilities: first, that the other person moves further away and, second, that the other person moves closer.

The situation most feared by pursuers is that if they pull back the other person will leave them or move further away. This fear is what keeps them pursuing and the relationship from moving in either direction. Unfortunately, there is never a *guarantee* that pulling back will make your relationship better. What it does do is help you to see the relationship more clearly and to see if there is any connectedness desired by the distancer. If your pursuit is the only energy being pumped into the relationship, then you may want to reassess how much longer you want to put your energy into a one-way relationship.

When the distancer moves further away, it usually occurs because the relationship has been one-sided for many years with the pursuing spouse being overly dependent upon the other person for his or her emotional needs. The pursuing spouse has counted too much on this relationship as a lifeline and this lifeline has succeeded in strangling the other person. Very often the pursuer in this position has cut off relationships and connections with his or her family of origin (parents and siblings).

If you think you want a more balanced relationship, then it

would be necessary to take the risk, pull back, and see what type of connectedness is left in the relationship. This is certainly a very difficult move to make, but the longer you wait to pull back the greater the chances are of driving the distancer further away.

Having the distancer move closer is the outcome that most pursuers would like but may never accomplish because of three reasons: One, they pull back only in hopes of getting the other to change and not because they see that they, in fact, need to make some serious changes to improve the relationship; two, they pull back but do not pull back far enough; and three, they are not patient enough to stick to the pulling back long enough for it to have an effect on the system. However, if these pitfalls can be avoided, then the flow or movement in the relationship system may begin to change. As long as the distancer feels the hands of the pursuer on him, he will never turn around and look back. He knows exactly where the pursuer is; he feels that if he stops distancing just for a second he will be consumed.

Before we can understand the movement of the distancer in response to the pulling back, let's examine how the pursuit is experienced and felt by the distancer. Figure 7-6 diagrams the "feel" of the pursuit on the distancer before the pursuer backed off. If the pursuer is able to give him some space, the distancer might begin to wonder where the pursuer is, since he no longer feels the pursuer breathing down his neck.

Figure 7-6

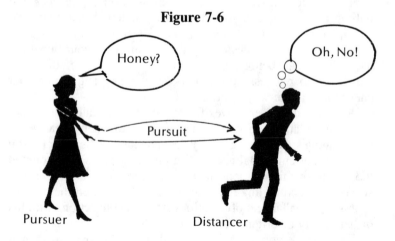

Figure 7-7 portrays this interaction with the man being the pursuer and with the rope symbolizing the tug that the distancer feels when being pursued. Distancers express fears of being "reined in" too tightly if they minimize the distance too much, whereas pursuers would say, "I just wanted to feel connected."

Figure 7-7

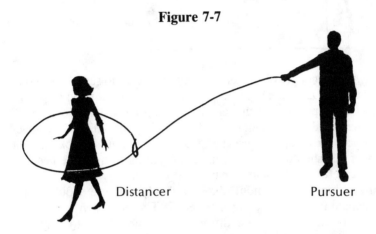

In Figure 7-8 the genogram suggests the pursuer has let go of the rope and taken her arms off the shoulders of the distancer; she has stopped pursuing and has begun to focus on herself. Now there is a change the distancer will feel. He may well have complained when the tug was there and will mention it when it is gone.

Figure 7-8

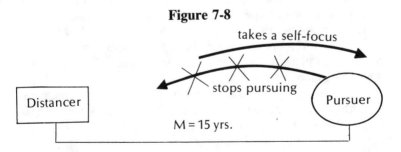

Let's take a look at how a husband, a pursuer, is trying to make some self-change in his relationship with his wife, a distancer (*Figure 7-9*).

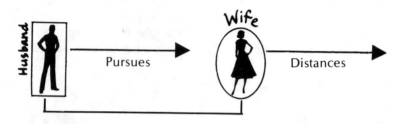

After a couple of weeks she might be heard to say, "How come you don't ask me about . . . [whatever the usual topic of pursuit has been between them] anymore? Don't you care about me?" Now the flow is changing and the wife, who has had her back turned for a "speedy escape" from his pursuit, is looking back over her shoulder to see what is happening to him. He needs to be careful not to start pursuing all over again just because she asked him this question. She is probably not sure about what is happening and is feeling threatened. The next step is to blame him because things are different. He should try to stay in a self-focus and tell her that he is working on getting his own "act" together by focusing on himself and trying not to change her. She may respond by saying, "Well, it's about time!" but he should try not to overreact to it because there is probably some truth to it. If she should ask more, he should be careful not to give her too much at one time about this change he's trying to make. She is not a feelings expert so he should be careful not to overwhelm her. Should she become more curious, she will ask again.

The more pursuers are able to pull back because they see that their behavior (pursuit) is part of the problem that keeps the relationship distant, the more space and change there is for the distancer to look over his or her shoulder, turn around, and begin to come closer. If that should happen, the flow of movement has been reversed in the twosome system; both are now behaving in a way that enables the once fixed distance (*Figure 7-10*) to be changed.

Both people will still have their tendencies to distance and pursue, especially during times of stress. Hopefully, the pursuer has learned that pursuing a distancer only created more distance. Before going on to take a look at how a distancer can change

Figure 7-10

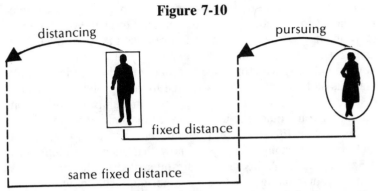

distancing

pursuing

fixed distance

same fixed distance

him/herself if desired, there is one more important point to be mentioned.

Avoid "Overloading" a Relationship. Pursuers often tend to overload and overintensify a particular relationship because they have allowed other significant relationships to deteriorate or be cut off. Therefore, one of the best ways not to overburden a relationship system is to keep the pathways open to your extended family network and close friends. This helps to avoid overloading the marriage relationship. The pursuer in Figure 7-11 is not only no longer pursuing her spouse but she is also working on improving her entire relationship system, especially connections to her family of origin.

Figure 7-11

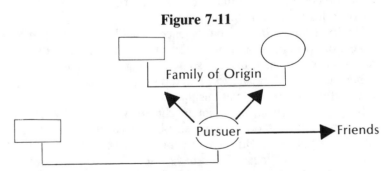

Family of Origin

Pursuer —————————▶ Friends

How a Distancer Can Work on Changing Self

After reviewing the "P and D" chart presented earlier, you may have recognized many of the characteristics of the distancing style of emotional interaction in yourself, such as you generally try to solve problems by yourself, you tend to prefer "alone" time in contrast to "together" time, or you tend to keep your feelings to yourself. You believe that you developed that style over time and you can trace it back into your family of origin. However, you are unhappy with this style of relating to others and you think that this style of interacting is related to your problem of feeling disconnected and isolated from your relationship network. You think that you would like to be more connected to the significant others in your life than you presently are, you are interested in making some changes and you know that change is defined as "changing self." Although you are interested in changing some part of your relating style, you are not quite sure how to begin and you think that change should be a gradual and evolving process.

It took time for your style to develop and it will take time and hard work for it to change. You were probably not aware of when and how your distancing style was developing but now that you have identified it and have decided that it is a problem for you, you are in a much better position to change it because of this awareness.

The Change Process. To start the process of self-change, the distancer must follow the same principle that applied to the pursuer, namely, to reverse the flow of movement in the relationship system. Just as the pursuer was coached to pull back, the distancer would be coached to gradually become a bit more involved and active in his or her relationship network.

(1) *The Change Itself.* The distancer would be encouraged to share more with the significant others in the relationship network: that is, share feelings, discuss some of what is happening in his or her life without having to be asked or questioned, and take a more active posture in relationships.

If you, as a distancer, want to change your style, you can consider a few of the following steps. Instead of waiting to be asked how you are feeling about something, perhaps you could volunteer your feelings. If you have a tendency to wait several days to talk about something that has you concerned, maybe you could shorten the time span a little bit and see how that feels. If you like a lot of "alone" time, maybe you could initiate a little more "together" time. Distancers sometimes have the impression that their significant other (usually a pursuer) knows them so well that they are able to read their minds. Take the crystal ball away and tell them a little of what is going on inside you. These are only a few beginning ideas for distancers who really want to change the space between themselves and others. Begin in moderation, expect that it will not proceed without some upset, and try not to get discouraged.

(2) *The system's reaction to the change.* The distancer is going to find himself or herself naturally resistant to share more of what is going on inside. This has been a pattern learned in the family of origin and practiced for years. The distancer might think "It is none of their business what is going on inside me . . . they really do not care anyway . . . they are only asking to be polite . . . I would have told them if they had just asked . . . besides, if they really cared about me they would know what I am thinking and how I am feeling" (the typical mind-reading assumption of distancers).

At this point, when the distancer encounters his or her own resistance to change, the distancer must ask the question,"Why do I really want to change?" There can be only one response if the process of self-change is to continue. "I am unhappy with my style of relating and with feeling disconnected from my relationship network. I am unhappy enough to stop blaming everyone else and work on my part in this problem."

Distancers will very often experience other types of resistance to change. They have had a history of not sharing a great deal and when they begin to change a little they could think that everyone else will know how tough it is for them and what a supreme effort they are making. However, their relationship network may not notice their attempts at self-change immediately, either because they have not been at it long enough or because they have not as yet been able to put enough of themselves into their relationships. The change will be noticed when it is steady and consistent.

Another resistance to change that the distancer may experience can come directly from the pursuer who has been presumably seeking such a change. Let's take the example given in Figure 7-12 (next page). Alice has been pursuing Harry for years to learn more about what is going on inside him, but he has always resisted, thinking of himself as the strong, silent type. Harry, however, decided that he did not feel as close to Alice as he would

Figure 7-12

like, so he decided that he would share more with Alice about how he was feeling and what worried him. It was his hope that this would cut down some of the distance that characterized their relationship.

Harry began telling Alice that he was depressed about having to work for the rest of his life and having to be the major financial support for their family. He really was dissatisfied with his job, but since it paid so well he felt that he could not change careers and do something that he would really enjoy. It was very difficult for Harry to start sharing this with Alice. Alice, who had been pursuing Harry, presumably to be in touch with this type of sharing, did not know how to deal with this change and began to distance from him. This upset Harry since he had expected the opposite from Alice. Her reaction could have slowed Harry's willingness to change. However, they were able to work it out by remembering that any change could be upsetting to the system—even change in a direction that everyone wanted. Alice was able to realize that Harry was finally sharing how he was feeling and not asking her to solve the problem for him. She had become overwhelmed because she felt that she had to have a solution rather than just be a supportive listener.

(3) *Dealing with the system's reaction to the change.* Figure 7-13 suggests avenues that Harry can follow as he tries to be more involved and connected in his relationship network. There will always be some resistance to change, either from self or from others in the system. The best way to deal with the resistance is to predict that it will come and then be prepared to deal with it. It never fails—everyone and every system resists change.

If the distancer is in a relationship with a pursuer (which is usually the case, since most two-person relationships have one person tending toward pursuing and the other tending toward

Figure 7-13

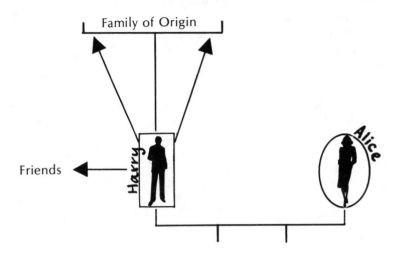

distancing), the pursuer might develop great expectations once some change begins to surface. If that happens, the distancer will probably back off, feeling that he or she cannot possibly meet the expectations. The distancer might believe that he or she is really making significant steps for someone who has not related in this way before, while the pursuer might look at it as "not enough" or "too little, too late." Both the distancer and the pursuer have to realize that any step taken by either of them to reverse the flow of motion in the relationship system is a step that is going to be hard. It will be going against the usual flow; therefore, it will feel uncomfortable and different.

Conclusion

Distancing and pursuing are two different sides to the same problem, that is, how to achieve the desired amount of closeness in a relationship. Neither is right or wrong; they both contribute to establishing imbalance in a relationship. As soon as one person begins to work on his or her part, change can occur.

187

References

Murray Bowen, *Family Therapy in Clinical Practice* (New York: Jason Aronson, 1978).

Thomas F. Fogarty, "The Distancer and the Pursuer," in *The Family*, Vol. 7, No. 1 (1979).

CHAPTER EIGHT

The Change Process
Applied to Triangles

HOW DOES our understanding of the change process within a family apply to triangles? As I have been saying, any one person can make a change in the family system by taking a different emotional position—changing self—and sticking to it in spite of the resistance to change that he or she experiences from others in the system. A triangle means that there are three dyads with problems, each of which must be approached separately to return the family to a higher level of functioning. A person must change his or her emotional position (from being too close or too distant) in each dyad.

In a sense, by discussing the path to closeness in the various dyads in the family, we have already seen how to achieve change in a triangle. Dyads typically handle difficulties by including a third person, object or issue as "the problem" between them. It follows that the way to handle a triangle is to work on the various one-to-one relationships within the triangle. Because change starts with the self, *and only the self*, if you are involved in a triangle the only change you have any control over is your involvement with each member of the various triangles in your family. You can expect that your changes will cause additional changes in the other one-to-one relationships in your family system, but you have no control over those changes.

The number of one-to-one relationships affected by any one change in any one family member adds up quickly. For example, in the case in Chapter 6, the most important triangle involved the husband, Joe, the wife, Bev, and the mother-in-law. The issue to Bev was spending more time alone with Joe and the kids, which meant spending less time with the mother-in-law. Right away, Bev's declaration that she would not spend the following Sunday with her mother-in-law affected numerous dyads. She had to deal with Joe's reaction, her mother-in-law's reaction and sit tight and observe Joe's reaction to his own mother. However, the two children jumped in, as well, and Bev found herself in a triangle with her son and her husband, with the issue being "keeping Dad happy." The daughter's comments about Grandma hint at another triangle issue. If Joe's unhappiness with her decision made him more testy, Bev might also have to sit by and watch him be less patient with the children. And, conceivably, the two children might be more argumentative with each other as family tension rises. So far, I count at least eight dyads affected by Bev's decision to cut down Sunday visits with Grandma. Some of these dyads are more important in the change process than others, but each has the power to rock the family boat.

I do not point out the resistance to change to make the task seem impossible; rather, I hope that, by showing the number of adjustments necessary to effect permanent change in the family system, you can understand why you find it difficult and why so many people wait until things are intolerable to make changes in their lives. In the short run, the status quo is always easier; it's the long run that we usually end up seeing as family therapists.

In therapy, the first step to working on a triangle is identifying the members of the triangle. Often the triangle involves a problem with a child's behavior. When a child is the focus of a triangle with his or her parents, it is the delicate task of the therapist to help the parents develop an approach to the child's problem, and to gently suggest that the parents address their own relationship as well. If the child is an adolescent, he or she will be much more involved in the treatment process, but a very basic assumption of family therapy is that the problem is not located in one person—it is in the system itself.

This brings us almost full circle. If you recall, in Chapter 1 the very basic idea of family therapy is that no one family member is "the problem." Still, by the time most families make it to family therapy, the idea that a child's problem could be a symptom of a larger problem in the family system is very threatening. Sometimes, each parent is perfectly willing to discuss his or her role in the child's problem, and can accept guidance on how to make changes in this area, but be oblivious to the difficulties in the marital relationship. These same parents may even be very open to discussing the difficulties they had as children, and what kind of parents they had, and still be reluctant to discuss the marital relationship.

These same parents may be even less willing to discuss their individual needs and wants for fear of opening a Pandora's Box of dissatisfaction with their own lives. Depending on the stage of life, an adult's individual concerns may be his or her career, personal health, how to balance success with enjoyment, spiritual fulfillment, or any number of other issues. Since each person's ability to achieve the things he or she wants from life is in some way tied to other members of the family system, to discuss one's dissatisfaction with the status quo means taking a risk. This is by no stretch of the imagination a plug for narcissism, but a critical part of happy family life is knowing what one wants as an individual. Setting realistic goals in one's personal life, seeing the way to achieve them, and being able to carry them out gives a person the inner strength needed to be a partner in the many dyads within the family system.

The triangle serves as a crutch for dissatisfaction within oneself, or dissatisfaction with an important dyad in the family. The goal of change is to work simultaneously on the surface problem at the same time one tries to address the long-standing problems that led to formulating a particular triangle. After identifying the members of the triangle, the next most important task is to focus on yourself and your own part in each one-to-one relationship. This involves pulling back and may be the hardest part of change, particularly if a child is involved. As parents we all feel that we have to protect our children, and it can be terribly hard to stand by and watch a youngster struggle with the other parent when that parent seems too domineering, or too distant, or too permissive, etc. Perhaps the best incentive for the well-meaning mother or father who wants to protect a child from the other parent's style is to recognize that by your interference you are blocking your child's chances of interacting and working out a relationship with the other parent.

An important note here. In this discussion I am not talking about cases of child abuse and neglect. Case histories of battered children usually reveal that one parent plays the role of the actual abuser, while the other parent collaborates by leaving the child alone with the abusive parent or covering up the abuse. Here, I am discussing the more normal differences in parenting philosophies, where one parent is likely to be more permissive (usually the mother) and the other parent tends to be a more strict disciplinarian.

Pulling back in other triangles means finding the strength to admit you have no control over an issue that may well affect your basic security. For example, if the triangle involves your spouse's job, it is useless to push the spouse to ask for more money or fewer responsibilities, even if those work-related problems seriously affect your spouse's personal happiness and, in turn, affect your marriage. You may wish your husband or wife were more relaxed about his or her job, but you cannot make it happen. The job may be an obstacle to your spending more time together, or pressures from the job may make him or her less pleasant to be around. However, a change in that area is ultimately in your spouse's control, not yours. It may be that your spouse's line of employment is not conducive to family life (e.g., medicine, armed services or sales) and that each of you have to reevaluate your personal priorities and your priorities as a couple, but each spouse must take responsibility for his or her own work and its problems.

This holds true for in-law problems as well. The issue is "Do you hold the Number 1 spot on your spouse's priority list?" and vice versa, and how do you show each other that. When in-laws interfere, they do so because that basic separation issue has not been resolved. You cannot separate your spouse from his or her parents—only your spouse can accomplish that. The separation process is something that happens inside a person, and trying to force your spouse away from his or her parents is like giving someone the answers on a test. He or she may pass the test and not learn a thing.

If an in-law problem involves your pulling back from your in-laws, you will also have to face their displeasure. You must be ready to be blamed if your spouse makes a change in his or her relationship with your in-laws. You don't have to relish their discomfort, just try to remember that it is much easier for them to blame you than to look at themselves, just as it is easier for you to blame them than it is to look at yourself. It may also help to imagine how you may feel in ten to twenty years when your children will leave home and marry, and there will be a few less faces at the dinner table.

Again, with alcohol, an affair, or outside activities, both people must take responsibility for their part in the problem. With alcohol, this means not collaborating by making excuses to employers and friends. With an affair, this means putting the focus on exploring the problems that led to the affair, and not on your partner's infidelity. With community activities, this means allowing the spouse to fulfill the outside commitments and placing your energy on renewing closeness in the dyad.

The risk is that when one does this, one opens up the possibility that there is not enough left in the marital dyad for it to survive. That scary thought alone keeps many people from getting out of triangles that make them very unhappy. Triangles provide a convenient dumping ground for anger. It's much easier to complain that your spouse's boss is an ogre than to confront your spouse with why he or she does not wish to spend more time with you. To take away your focus on the spouse's job, or his or her parents, or an affair, means opening up to some very difficult realizations about yourself and the marriage. You must also accept the fact that if you take your energy away from the surface issue and refocus on the "real issues," your spouse may not be quite ready to join you.

While searching for these real issues, it is often interesting to note that what gets you so upset about the other person or persons in the triangle may be hitting closer to home than you think. In other words, if you are very upset about your partner's alcohol consumption (assuming he or she is not an alcoholic), chances are there is something about drinking itself that disturbs you. Perhaps it is someone in your family of origin whose drinking problem still upsets you and, not having worked that out, every time you see your spouse look at the Scotch you get upset. If the problem is with an in-law situation, perhaps your reactivity and upset is stirred because it reminds you of a loyalty issue that occurred in your family while growing up.

In a child-focused triangle, both parents have an intense emotional involvement with the same person, the child. Although each parent may try to pull back from the child's relationship with the other parent and refocus energy on the marriage, it may be more difficult to do so than with other triangles. After all, the other one-to-one relationship involved goes on right under your nose and the kind of involvement that goes on between a parent and child is unique.

If you look back, a majority of the case examples have involved triangles with children. The vignette below capsulizes the general issues involved in changing the one-to-one relationships between a mother, father and son. This imaginary family system contains only three people, but the situation has the potential to become quite complicated. Each of the three dyads contains two people, each with a different point of view about the various relationships. In order to shift this triangle back to a more healthy position, each member has to face up to working on two relationships at the same time.

Figure 8-1 illustrates this common triangle that often occurs between parent and a child. There are many reasons that could have led to this overclose mother-son relationship; for example, the father was overinvolved in his job or drank too much, but the real problem would lie in the relationship system between the husband and wife. They were unable to develop the emotional closeness that both needed in their relationship so, rather than face that issue directly, they avoided it and hoped that things would calm down. As we know, it seldom works that way.

Figure 8-1

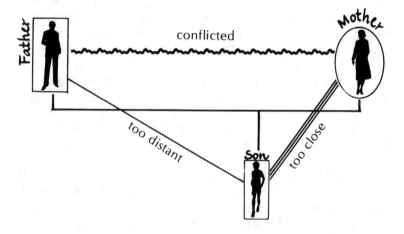

This family triangle has become a closed system. There is a fixed distance between the three members. Father knows that Son is his mother's boy, and Mother does not expect Father to fulfill her emotional needs for closeness. Son enjoys his exalted role as Mother's favorite. No matter who makes a move, he or she can expect the other members to react strongly. If Father suddenly takes a romantic turn and suggests a weekend alone with Mother, the Son would probably act out. If Son tried to move closer to Father, Mother might express feelings of rejection. If Mother moved closer to Son than she is already, the Father may act out his jealousy by becoming harsh with the child. There are any number of possibilities of how any one person's move toward another will upset the closed system. In a closed system, members feel that there is a limited amount of intimacy available. They assume that a move closer to one member means depriving some other member of closeness.

The goal is to create an open system where members expect closeness to be more fluid and to be a function of individual need and circumstances. Individuals in an open system can have several one-to-one relationships with members in the same family without affecting other one-to-one relationships. Figure 8-2 represents an open system where people have a high degree of autonomy, self-determination and freedom to move in the relationship system. The absence of connecting lines indicates the openness, so opposed to the various symbols used to describe less fluid relationships. The total capacity for closeness is not fixed.

Figure 8-2

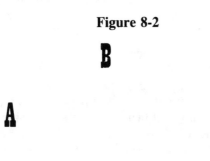

If A moves closer to B, nothing is taken away from C; C does not feel left out, and B does not feel invaded.

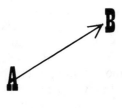

If C distances from both A and B, A and B do fine separately and together.

When C moves closer to B, A is not jealous and does not feel excluded.

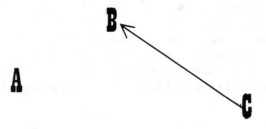

Everyone in this open system is free to determine his or her own one-to-one relationship. This is what we should be striving toward in our relationship system—person-to-person relationships that do not emotionally pull in a third person. It is a process of striving. It is difficult to get there because relationships are fluid and in constant motion. To be in an effective communications system means a commitment to a lifelong process of working on the triangles in significant relationships and avoiding the stranglehold they form around close and intense relationships.

How could one de-triangle (change) the imaginary closed system depicted in Figure 8-1? There are many ways to approach the de-triangling process but it is always best to start with the person who seems most willing to change or make a different move. In this case let's say that the Mother is seeking help because the Son is beginning to get in trouble with the police and the Father doesn't seem to care. Mother appears the one most willing at this point to do something different. However, that may be because she sees the problem as outside of herself and as being in her husband and son.

Let's assume that this family is willing to come in and be involved in counseling. Since Mother has initiated the request for help, I would ask her to make the first shift to improve the family balance. Mother would need to de-intensify her relationship with the Son . . . or increase the space between herself and her Son. Mother will probably say at this point, "Why must I go first? My husband is the problem. If I back off one inch our Son will think nobody cares about him." Notice how easy it is to blame and how much resistance there is to change even from the one who asks for the help.

Assuring her that the child would not be neglected when she backs off, I would simultaneously ask Father to move in and become more involved with the Son. There is absolutely no way that Father could move closer to the Son as long as Mother has all the space filled up. Father will probably have some reason for why he is unable to move closer to Johnny—such as, he's too busy at work; Johnny's hair is too long, etc. This should not be seen as Father's not caring, but as a combination of Father's resistance to change and his unfamiliarity with a new role. Father will need a little coaching on how to move in because it will be a new role for him to fill. The Son may predictably resist the family shift by telling his traditionally distant father to "get lost," as Father tries to follow the counselor's suggestion to become more involved. Father should be cautioned not to become discouraged if this occurs, since the child has been feeling abandoned by him for some time; a better relationship in the long run will require effort and a willingness to risk getting hurt. Figure 8-3 (next page) shows the initial shift in the triangle (as compared with Figure 8-1) as the relationships between Father and Son and Mother and Son slowly change. Note also that Mother and Father's relationship becomes less conflictual as they gain a better perspective on how to parent their child. While the triangle shifts gradually, all three people in this triangle will experience anxiety.

As you remember, change is a three-step process: first, there is the change or the taking of a new position; second, there is the family's reaction to the change—as expressed by Mother, Father and Son in the above vignette—and third, there is the need to move through the family's reaction to the change.

There are several points that need to be kept in mind as this family triangle begins to change. Mother, who has had her own

Figure 8-3

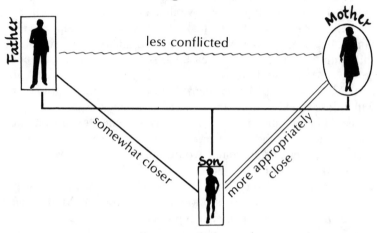

way of being involved with her Son, will be tempted to try to get Father to parent the boy the way she thinks it should be done. (But please, Mom, if you really want things to change, stay out of your husband and Johnny's one-to-one!) The second point also involves Mother. Since she has been the one most involved with the child, she is going to find it difficult to back off because she has been devoting a good deal of her emotional energy to him instead of to her husband. What is Mother to do with all the time, worry, energy and emotional involvement that used to go toward the boy?

As Mother de-intensifies her involvement with her Son, she needs to increase her connectedness with her husband and other members of her family system. Whenever a person has an over-close or overintense relationship with one member in a family, there are usually other relationships in the system which have deteriorated and become dysfunctional, conflictual or completely cut off. When other emotional lifelines are cut off or are in poor working order, there is a tendency to overload the ones presently in existence.

In addition to the work that Mother must do, Father has to take a look at why he is so removed from his wife and why he is distant from his Son. There is a lot of work to be done if Father would like to improve his connections to both. One would also wonder what type of relationships Father has with his extended family. He seems, in this example, to be somewhat isolated. If that is the case, it would be important for Father to work on opening up those ties to his family of origin.

Figure 8-4

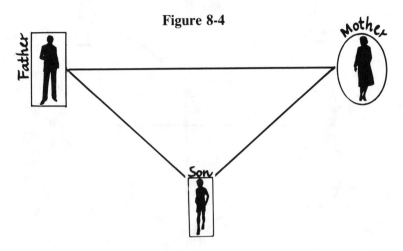

Finally, the Son needs to work on developing a one-to-one relationship with each parent. He must avoid taking sides or allowing either of his parents to use him as an emotional substitute for what is missing in their marital relationship. The older the child the more consciously involved he or she can be in the change process.

Figure 8-4 indicates that the above suggestions were followed by Mother, Father and the Son and the triangle is in much better balance and the relationships are much more equal.

Improve Relationships with Extended Family

Since triangles form when relationships become too intense, it would be crucial for this family to increase their emotional connectedness with as many members of the family system as possible. If one has strong extended family relationships, then one will make fewer demands, thus placing less stress on one's nuclear family relationships. With this in mind, Figure 8-5 shows this family moving back up their family tree to improve their connectedness with family members as well as reaching out to make and improve relationships in their social and friendship network.

Figure 8-5

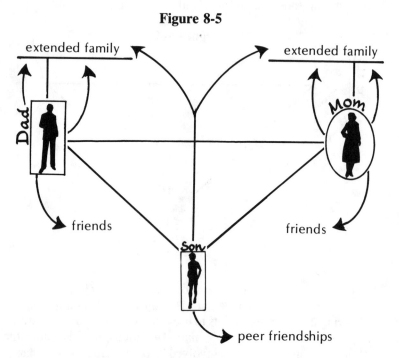

If one of your triangles involves your in-laws, it may be time to take a close look at your relationships with your own family of origin. If your spouse is overly close to his or her parents, the primary issue may be the marriage, but a second issue would be how you feel about your own parents. If the problem is an interfering mother-in-law, you need to ask yourself why she is so annoying to you. It could be that your own mother is also very interfering, or it could be that she is quite distant. You may not have ever questioned how your mother treated you until you came into close contact with your spouse's mother and a completely different style of parenting. It may actually be that anyone in their right mind would agree that your mother-in-law is a pest, but you still can't change that. You can help yourself by taking your energy away from your spouse's relationship with his/her mother and by beginning to work on your relationship with your own parents.

Many clients at first resist working on relationships with their parents, saying that the older generation will never change, etc. Some may assume that by becoming an adult the relationship with the parents somehow reaches the end of its progress. However, as we have already seen, all relationships are constantly changing, just as surely as the people in the relationships are constantly changing. True, some things about us may be relatively stable—a sense of humor, or a tendency to have a quick temper. But the way we exist in our daily lives changes as we change jobs, have children, learn new skills, meet new people, and think new ideas. Countless things influence our lives and our relationships and influence our parents and siblings as well.

What happens in relationships with our families of origin is that we often avoid discussing the very real changes we experience in ourselves as individuals and continue to act out old family routines. One 36-year-old corporate lawyer I know, hating to go to holiday dinners because his two older brothers still teased him and put him down the way they did when he was 4, decided to boycott. But rather than deprive himself of the joy of spending the holidays with family, something he really wants, he would be better off to devise a plan of how he could become less reactive to the old family script and learn a new way of enjoying himself with family. His brothers are not going to change first, and certainly not while they can still get a rise out of him. When the script is long-standing and the emotional intensity high, you may need a family therapist to help you think out a plan to make your well-intentioned visits produce more satisfaction.

Much of the discomfort in relationships with extended family comes from feeling hooked to remain in some outdated role. It could be a functional role, such as the middle-aged man in Chapter 5, George Brown, Jr., who still felt responsible for taking care of his mother and her home. Or it could be an emotional role like the young lawyer above, who was always "the fool" in any family situation. Either way, it's a difficult position. Having too much unresolved family baggage can overload an already busy and stressful life, and being caught (and collaborating) in the role of family scapegoat, when one goes through daily life having respect from peers and clients, can make an otherwise pleasant time perfectly dreadful.

Whatever the problem, ignoring it does not make it go away. Cutoffs and boycotts deny the emotional support we all need. Working it out provides the kind of satisfaction that only achieving a renewed closeness with a family member can do for the heart. Bonds with close friends are valuable but somehow they also seem optional. Our families are supposed to love us and we are supposed to love them. In a crisis, most of us turn to our families and, if we cannot do so, we feel a double pain—the crisis itself and the feeling that those we love are not there for us. Good relationships outside of your family system never take the place of family relationships. This is why family therapists always encourage family members to work at improving their connections within their family system. This is also why cutoffs between family members are never the solution to a problem. Some connection is better than no connection at all. Thus, when a person is asked by a family therapist to do some work on improving his or her relationships with parents and family of origin, one often hears, "My parents are hopeless . . . I couldn't talk to them when I was a kid so how could it be possible now?" Family systems do not work this way; you do not leave your family behind you. The above statement fails to take into account the emotional inter-connectedness of family members over time and the inter-generational passage of family patterns.

Let's compare the family emotional system to an electrical circuit and then to a human heart. An electrical circuit works best when all wires are connected and the transfer of current is flowing smoothly through the system. When some of the wires go bad or a few connectors snap, certain connectors have to carry the whole load and a great deal of pressure is put on a few connections, overloading the system. This sometimes results in a blowout! With the human heart, if veins or arteries get blocked or clogged, it puts tremendous stress on the other connectors, causing massive strokes and heart attacks. When the connectors are blocked or not functioning adequately, all the parts of the body system suffer because they are not being properly nourished. These analogies to electrical circuitry and the human heart can give you a good idea of what happens when there are breakdowns, blocks, and cutoffs in the family's emotional system.

Focusing on relationships with extended family helps put the marriage in perspective. Too often, people experience intense difficulties with their parents as children and adolescents and bring to marriage the high expectation that "Now, at last, I will have a happy home." Such a marriage carries a heavy emotional burden above and beyond the normal task of developing a marriage—making an unhappy person happy. Sometimes young couples move away from parents, thinking this will help. On the contrary, it may make things worse. There may actually be more fights between couples at a distance from their parents because of this unfinished business with parents. This is because anger as a feeling does not have any control over itself. If it's there it comes out. The goal is to direct it in the right place so that it does not disrupt other relationships. By continuing to work on relationships with parents and siblings, you can actually relieve some of the stress on the marriage by not blaming the spouse for all of your problems.

There are many possible triangular situations that can occur in families, but the same general principles apply to all. Try to keep these points in mind when thinking about how to get out of a triangle:

(1) The triangle has formed because a dyad or one-to-one relationship has become too stressful for the twosome to talk openly or deal directly with each other.

(2) Both members of the twosome have covertly agreed to choose a third person or object to focus on that allows for some cooling off but never gets to the real issue between the twosome.

(3) By taking the focus off the third part of the triangle, that is, the concentration on the mother-in-law, the alcoholism, or whatever, the twosome has to look at what is happening between themselves instead of outside themselves. This is certain, in the beginning, to increase the stress between the twosome but it is the only way to improve or change the relationship. Change can only occur when you talk about the issue instead of the symptom.

(4) When you get to the point of knowing that you are fighting about a symptom or the third part of a triangle, that's progress. However, sometimes we get so emotionally involved in a triangle that we can't figure out the issue. A good family thera-

pist can help a family clear the confusion and identify the real issue.

(5) Remember that it only takes one person to change his/her position for the triangle to begin to shift.

Conclusion

THE PURPOSE of this book has been to pass on a body of knowledge about families that has been in the possession of family therapists but not readily available to families. It is hoped that the reader obtained a basic knowledge of Family Systems Theory so that he/she is better able to understand family functioning in general and his/her family in particular in order that family problems might be prevented and family stress reduced.

This book has given you a basic knowledge of Family Systems Theory upon which to build as you pass through the Family Life Cycle. It has not covered—nor was it the author's intention to cover—some particularly stressful areas which many families are facing today: for example, separation, divorce, single parenthood, remarriage, serious illness, and death. It is the author's hope to address these topics in a second book devoted specifically to these pressing issues. The concepts that have been discussed in this book lay the crucial groundwork for one to gain a fuller understanding of these latter issues.

Hopefully, *Family Matters: A Layperson's Guide to Family Functioning* has increased your awareness of and hope for family life. If it has, please pass along your optimism, enthusiasm, and a copy of this book to others.